CONTENTS

Introduction

C P Snow's statement in a BBC broadcast in 1936 that he saw 'modern advertising as an attempt to impel people to buy, what if it were not for the advertisement, they would never think of buying', (Nevett, 1982, p.161) is only partially applicable to the advertising of cosmetics. Since earliest times, women have decorated their faces and bodies. The twentieth-century cosmetics advertising industry aimed to sell women an ideal image of themselves and a lifestyle by the use of association and persuasion. It also strove to develop and maintain brand loyalty in a hugely competitive market.

This brief history of twentieth-century printed advertising of cosmetics goes from the early part of the century, when there were few advertisements, through the years of mass-circulation magazines with considerable advertising space to the beginning of the twenty-first century, when vast numbers of printed advertisements have to compete with those in other media such as television, cinema and the Internet.

This book covers advertisements of women's cosmetics for the face and hands – foundations, creams and powders, eye shadow and mascara, lipstick and nail varnish. Although there are only a few basic cosmetic products, there are numerous companies advertising all their different brands and colours through campaigns aimed mainly at women. These Library of Historic Advertising advertisements appeared in both British and

There is only one

Pan-Cake Make-Up...the original

created by *Max Factor Hollywood*

★ *It creates a lovely new complexion*

★ *It helps conceal tiny complexion faults*

★ *It stays on for hours without re-powdering*

Look for a lovelier *you* when you look in your mirror after your very first make-up with "Pan-Cake". You'll see for yourself how "Pan-Cake" gives your skin a softer, smoother, younger look, how it helps conceal tiny complexion faults, stays on for hours without re-powdering...yes, does everything you've always wanted make-up to do. So, make up with "Pan-Cake" today...you, like millions, will instantly approve this new make-up fashion.

Judy Garland

starring in Metro-Goldwyn-Mayer's

"THE HARVEY GIRLS"

A Technicolor Musical

Pan-Cake* Make-Up

AN EXCLUSIVE FORMULA PROTECTED BY U. S. PATENT NOS. 2034697-2101834

* Pan-Cake ...Trade Mark Reg. U.S. Pat. Off.

ORIGINATED BY MAX FACTOR HOLLYWOOD

ILLUSTRATION 1a

1945

YARDLEY SHOOT NOTES

Tuesday 9am

Remember to match
    lips & nails

all have
Camellia Extract
(+ v. moisturising)

Keep the look
soft & classic

YARDLEY
LIPS & NAILS
CARE & COLOUR COMBINED

ILLUSTRATION 1b
Vogue, 1994

American magazines, since the majority of the cosmetics companies are international in scope.

There are five main themes running throughout the history of cosmetics advertising:

- The change of advertising target from upper-class women at the beginning of the century to women of all social classes as cosmetics became not only more available but also more affordable
- Advertising aimed at women who wanted 'to catch a man'
- Older women who could look younger and more beautiful if they used a particular cosmetic brand
- The arrival of financially independent women in the workforce, adding to the existing market of married women reliant on their husbands' income
- Influence of cinema from the 1930s onwards to sell products to make women as glamorous as the stars endorsing the products.

Added to these five themes are two later developments:

- Development and growth of the teenage market from the 1970s onwards when magazine buying was enormous
- The inclusion of women of colour in advertisements and, since the 1990s, the development of products specially for these women.

The majority of the advertisements illustrated conform to a basic format throughout the century. They usually show white, slightly older women in close up, wearing the products, sometimes in settings (romantic or fantasy), looking either directly at the reader or into the middle distance. The aim is to get the reader to buy the product because she is led to believe that she could look and feel as glamorous as the model wearing the product(s) in the advertisements. Max Factor in the 1930s and 1940s used Hollywood stars to endorse his products, which had started life as cinema make-up. Judy Garland is only one such example **ILLUSTRATION 1a**. The trend continues even into this century with Helena Bonham Carter as the face of Yardley **ILLUSTRATION 1b**. Cosmetic products could also help women look younger and more beautiful (Helena Rubinstein, Estée Lauder, Elizabeth Arden and Oil of Ulay) or help them 'catch a man'.

Although there is an element of sexual allure in many of the advertisements, especially those for lipsticks, sex became more overt from the 1950s onwards, especially during and after the 1970s feminist era, when women wanted to look good for themselves, rather than necessarily to ensnare a man.

Each chapter covers a decade, (apart from 1900 to 1930, when cosmetics advertising was in its infancy) to the end of the century when the advertising of hundreds of cosmetic products continues to dominate the current mass media.

Chapter 1

1900–1930

Flappers and film stars

During the first two decades of the twentieth century, cosmetics were mainly made and used at home by older women, for whom 'society might give its approval to the use of powder and rouge… but unmarried girls were expected to rely on the natural attributes of an unpainted complexion' (Gunn, 1973, p.142). Most upper-class women made (or had their maids make) their own cosmetic preparations and working-class women did not have access to such products. The only other members of society using cosmetics at this time were actresses and prostitutes. Since there was therefore a limited product range and market, there was very little advertising. The few that did appear did so as small ads in respectable magazines.

With the greater acceptance of cosmetics usage, influenced partly by Diaghilev's use of them in his ballets, advertisements started to appear in magazines, such as those for Madame Helena Rubinstein's luxury products. Her first British beauty salon opened in London in 1908 for women from the upper echelons of society. These early advertisements were in the form of testimonials from actresses and society women. In the *Play Pictorial* of 1911, a full-page advertisement features two such women who use Rubinstein's 'specialities for home treatment, intended for every requirement of the complexion [which] are now found on the dressing tables of fashionable and fastidious women all over the world'.

Women who use Pond's
The Business Girl

Occupations that necessitate much time being spent indoors are not good for the complexion. It is therefore no wonder that the modern business girl is a staunch advocate of the use of the two purest and popular creams—Pond's Vanishing Cream and Pond's Cold Cream.

Pond's Vanishing Cream—for day use—being non-greasy, requires no massage, but disappears instantly into the skin, leaving no trace of use. It is a protective cream against the elements, making the complexion delicate and appealingly soft and smooth at all times.

Pond's Cold Cream—a food and cleanser for tired pores—should be gently massaged into the face, neck, hands and arms each night on retiring. Because it supplements the natural oil of the skin it aids in preventing and eradicating the little lines that time and care are constantly trying to etch around the eyes and mouth. Pond's Creams never promote the growth of hair.

"TO SOOTHE AND SMOOTH YOUR SKIN."

Both Creams of all Chemists and Stores in handsome opal jars, 1/3 and 2/6. Also collapsible tubes 7½d. (handbag size) and 1/-.

POND'S EXTRACT CO. (Dept. 140), 71, Southampton Row, London, W.C.1.

POND's Cold Cream and Vanishing Cream

ILLUSTRATION 2

1912

ILLUSTRATION 3

The Strand Magazine, 1925

With World War One and the subsequent social changes, including greater female emancipation, there was a growth in the use of cosmetics by women of all social classes. Working-class and society women started wearing cosmetics as the stigma attached to them from the last decades had disappeared after the end of the war. This growth of the beauty industry together with the simultaneous one in women's magazines, contributed to the development of the printed advertising of cosmetics.

Pond's, founded in America in 1846, like Rubinstein, used actresses and dancers to promote its cold and vanishing creams, but also had its Pond's girl campaigns, beginning in 1904. One of them was 'The Business Girl' 1912, **ILLUSTRATION 2** showing a woman answering a phone in an office, which is one of the earliest examples of an advertisement featuring women in the workforce in the LHA collection. The woman uses Pond's vanishing cream to make 'her complexion delicate and appealingly soft and smooth at all times'.

Advertisements of this period were mainly in black and white and tended to consist of descriptions of the products and what they could do for the women who used them.

After the end of World War One the changes in British society contributed to an increased use of cosmetics by women from all social classes. It was now deemed socially acceptable to be seen outdoors wearing make-up.

ILLUSTRATION 4
Punch, 1927

Women had been given the vote and the 1920s was the era of the 'flappers' – young women wishing to enjoy themselves and shock their elders by rebelling against the social norms of the post-war period. At the same time, following Helena Rubinstein's example, Elizabeth Arden (her arch rival) opened a beauty salon in London in 1922 and Estée Lauder one in Paris. These salons all promoted the idea of women becoming beautiful and looking younger if they used their products. New mass-produced cosmetic products together with an increase in the number of women's magazines meant also growth in the advertising of these products.

A Pond's colour advertisement of 1925 **ILLUSTRATION 3** has an image of a young woman, her social class indicated by her sumptuous fur and gloves, making reference in the text to Pond's advertisements of the previous decade for its Cold and Vanishing creams. Two years later in a Punch advertisement **ILLUSTRATION 4** a slightly older woman of the same social class shows off her smooth skin contrasted with a prickly rose. It is worth mentioning that in both these advertisements the products are displayed in exactly the same way. The Pond's girl advertising campaign of this decade involved the story of a young girl as she matured into a young married woman. For example one advertisement shows her engaged and lovely and all because she uses Pond's creams.

ILLUSTRATION 5

1920

Reproduced courtesy of Coty Inc.

The 1920s saw the introduction from Paris to Britain of mass-produced lipstick, the increased use of mascara (formerly used only as stage make-up) and nail varnish. Cutex was one of the earliest companies producing and advertising its nail varnish, which during the 1920s was called Liquid Polish. Bold, bright colours appeared later in the century. The 1920 advertisement **ILLUSTRATION 5** simply shows a woman's hands applying the nail varnish with details of how to look after her nails. It's in black and white and the product is included in the advertisement. In contrast, a 1929 Cutex advertisement **ILLUSTRATION 6** has an image of a woman in one of London's smartest restaurants, Gennaro's. Her hand is shown removing the cherry from her drink. The caption is 'Cutex Liquid Polish' but the product itself is not shown. The implied message is that if you wear this nail varnish you can improve your chances of 'catching a man' and becoming more socially upwardly mobile.

Maybelline, founded in 1915 in America and branded in 1920, concentrated on mascara, which contrasted with Cutex and its nail varnish. The advertisements promoted the idea that if you wore Maybelline, you could be as beautiful as the film stars, for example Phyllis Haver. This is an early example of the use of personalities to sell cosmetics – an idea which was fully developed in the following decades. The end of the era saw the stock market crash of 1929 and the start of the 1930s Depression.

ILLUSTRATION 6

1929

Chapter 2

1930s

A golden age

After the end of the Depression, there was a transformation of cosmetics advertising into what was considered by some to be a golden age of advertising. Not only was there a huge variety of products for sale, but they were of better quality and had become more affordable by all social classes. Cosmetics had also become an antidote to the depression years and so advertising agencies used this together with a growth in the number of women's magazines to advertise their cosmetic products.

Max Factor & Company, established in 1909, which opened its first salon in London in 1936, was a provider of make-up to the Hollywood stars. The firm's founder Max Factor took the opportunity, with the development of colour cinema film, to use Hollywood stars such as Jean Harlow and later Lana Turner and Judy Garland, to endorse and sell his foundations to women with social aspirations ILLUSTRATION 1a (see page 5). His message was simple – if you use Max Factor products, you too could look as glamorous as the stars. Elizabeth Arden also used this method in an advertisement of 1937 featuring Janet Gaynor ILLUSTRATION 7. The message is clear with the caption 'It could happen to YOU' plus the copy 'every star…every movie fan…*every woman* who ever dreamed to possess glamour, may share in the discovery of Screen and Stage make-up by Elizabeth Arden…that they may find, thrill and believe in their own beauty'.

Janet Gaynor as she appears in "A Star is Born"

ILLUSTRATION 7
1937

"It Could Happen to YOU!"

THE very heart and soul of Hollywood is spoken in those few words . . . words that have brought a thousand Cinderellas to Hollywood and made stars of them.

Elizabeth Arden has used her Screen and Stage Make-Up in David O. Selznick's revealing story of "A Star is Born" to dramatize truly the transformation of grey Esther Blodgett (Janet Gaynor) into glamorous Vicki Lester (Janet Gaynor).

Most Importantly . . . . .

So successful have the stars found the new Elizabeth Arden Technicolor make-up for the screen that they have taken it up in private life, creating a vogue for the subtle coloring offered only by Elizabeth Arden.

Every star . . . every movie fan . . . *every woman* who ever dreamed to possess glamour, may share in the discovery of Screen and Stage Make-Up by Elizabeth Arden . . . that they may find, thrill and believe in their own beauty, and like the people of stage and screen, live the days and nights of their private lives in rich fulfillment.

PRICE LIST

Foundations . . Nos. 1 to 10 (Screen);
  1x to 20x (Stage) $1.00
Lipsticks . . convenient swivel top . . . $1.00
Liners . . 1x to 15x (Screen and Stage) $1.00
Powder . . Nos. 1 to 10 (Screen);
  1x to 16x (Stage) $1.00
Remover . . (Screen and Stage) $1.00

And a complete group of theatrical preparations designed by Elizabeth Arden — sold by exclusive Elizabeth Arden retail distributors everywhere. The booklet "Professional Information" B-1, may be obtained by writing Screen and Stage Make-Up Laboratories: 5533 Sunset Blvd., Hollywood, Calif.

SCREEN and STAGE MAKE-UP

by

Elizabeth Arden

Special Offer:

Buyers of any $5 combination of Elizabeth Arden Screen and Stage Make-Up preparations will receive free one handsome, mirrored make-up kit as illustrated above, and similar to those used by Hollywood stars.

Farewell to Age!

ILLUSTRATION 8

1936

*" Grow young along with me,
the best is yet to be ! "*

. . . E L I Z A B E T H   A R D E N

You who value beauty, promise yourself to treat your face like a pearl of great price. Morning and night cleanse with Venetian Cleansing Cream and Ardena Skin Tonic which work together as one to keep your complexion clear and soft. And then, to keep the texture smooth and fine, pat on Velva Cream ; or, if you're inclined toward dryness, use Orange Skin Food instead.

Then, at least three times a week, lift your beauty to new heights with Velva Cream Masque. It will pick up the least suspicion of a droop at the corners of your mouth and whisk away puffs under your eyes and refine relaxed pores. Your face will be remodelled, aglow, and smoother than it has ever felt before.

And finally achieve a new complexion with Elizabeth Arden's two-powder technique that makes an ordinary make-up look as dowdy as last year's hat. Use Ardena Powder, then dust over with Japonica Powder to give your skin a porcelain smooth finish that lasts all day without repowdering. Because one application lasts so long you use much less powder than usual and look the lovelier for it.

Venetian Cleansing Cream liquefies instantly and cleanses superbly, and should be used with the Skin Tonic. They work together as one . . . 4/6 to 22/6

Ardena Skin Tonic removes every trace of cream without drying the skin. It tones, clears and brightens the skin . . . 3/6 to 75/-

Velva Cream Masque smooths out lines, refines the pores and brings out your natural sparkling colour . . . 21/-

Ardena Velva Cream is an outstanding emollient, soothing and gratifying, ideal for young skins . . . 4/6 to 22/6

Orange Skin Food should be used by every woman over thirty to combat dryness, prevent lines and help to keep a smooth skin . . . 4/6 to 35/-

Elizabeth Arden's new complexion. Ardena Powder, 7/6 and 12/6, smoothed over with Japonica Powder in a slightly different shade . . . 12/6

Send for Miss Arden's Instruction Book, which contains the answer to every beauty problem.

Elizabeth Arden
Elizabeth Arden Ltd.

LONDON 25 OLD BOND STREET W1

NEW YORK : *Elizabeth Arden I.A* • PARIS : *Elizabeth Arden S.A.* • ROME : *Elizabeth Arden S.A.I.* • BERLIN : *Elizabeth Arden G.m.b.H.* • HOLLYWOOD : *3933 Wiltshire Blvd.*

One of Elizabeth Arden's advertising slogans was for older women who could look younger if they used her products ILLUSTRATION 8. 'Farewell to Age! Grow young along with me, the best is yet to be!' shows an image of lilies and a Madonna-type woman, whose beautiful features were acquired by the application of various creams, especially 'Orange Skin Food', which should be used by every woman over thirty. No actual products are displayed, just the effect they would have on older women (see Pond's ILLUSTRATION 2). Elizabeth Arden's Colour Harmony product range continues this method of showing a glamorous woman wearing Redwood lipstick, rouge and nail varnish (latter not visible) with no sign of the products or their packaging ILLUSTRATION 9.

THE MODERN WOMAN — ELIZABETH ARDEN'S MASTERPIECE

Naturalness is the keynote of the new collections, with their engaging feminine lines and girlish silhouettes . . . What colour could be more natural and yet more subtle than Elizabeth Arden's fascinating **REDWOOD**, her latest contribution to the all-important science of Colour Harmony? . . . This soft but glowing shade makes a perfect accompaniment to the new mimosa yellows, cinnamon browns, ambers, delicate coral and cool sea-green . . . For the more dramatic blues and mauvish pinks (also featured prominently in the Paris collections) she sponsors **SKYBLUE PINK** — a brilliant newcomer : while her famous and delightful **PEONY** still holds its own . . . Colour Harmony completes the contemporary masterpiece.

REDWOOD MAKE-UP : *Redwood Lipstick, Rouge, Nail Varnish*
SKYBLUE PINK MAKE-UP : *Skyblue Pink Lipstick, Rouge, Nail Varnish*
PEONY MAKE-UP : *Peony Lipstick, Rouge, Nail Varnish*

Elizabeth Arden

Elizabeth Arden Ltd

2 5   O L D   B O N D   S T R E E T   L O N D O N   W 1

ILLUSTRATION 9

Harper's Bazaar, 1939

Natural lipstick
Natural, Rose or
Mauve polish

Coral lipstick
Coral polish

Cardinal lipstick
Cardinal polish

Ruby lipstick
Ruby polish

TODAY YOUR LIPSTICK
MUST MATCH YOUR NAIL POLISH

Cutex presents
a complete range of matching Lipsticks and Nail Polishes

CUTEX has started a brand-new, interesting vogue in make-up! They're giving you a complete set of Cutex Lipsticks to match and tone in with their nail polishes!

So no more ugly clashing of purple-red lips and yellow-red finger tips in your close-ups. Perfect harmony from now on!

Cutex Ruby Lipstick—the identical rich red of your Cutex Ruby nails.

Cutex Cardinal Lipstick—the color twin for Cutex Cardinal Polish.

Cutex Coral Lipstick—just the right lovely color tone for Cutex Coral nails.

Cutex Natural Lipstick is not only a magnificent match for Cutex Mauve nails, but goes perfectly with Cutex Natural Polish and Cutex Rose Polish.

So there you are—all set! And you can't murmur about the cost of this new matching lip-

stick idea, because you get these Cutex sticks for only 50 cents. Half the price you usually pay! Yet the new Cutex Lipstick has all the grand quality you would find at twice the price!

Easy to spread . . . and won't dry your lips

Try the new Cutex Lipstick. It's creamy like velvet! . . . but not greasy. It's nice and permanent. And it goes on like a dream!

Be one of the first to follow this new matching lips and nail tips vogue!

Cutex Liquid Polish—Crème or Clear—35¢ a bottle, and the new matching Cutex Lipsticks, only 50¢ a stick.

NORTHAM WARREN
New York, Montreal, London, Paris

Perfect harmony between your lips and finger tips

ILLUSTRATION 10
1935

NEW SETTINGS BY NATURE

NEW FACES BY YARDLEY!

The smart summer audience of 1936 has elected to seek much of its entertainment out-of-doors. And out-of-doors one follows them to seek a beauty miracle in women's faces. For mingling with the jewelled, englamoured throng at Glyndebourne's lovely Mozart shrine . . . swept with the laughing crowd through Malvern, or at Regent's Park, one notices an identical phenomenon, they say.

It is this: <u>There are no more old or ugly women!</u>

We like to think that the explanation of this apparent miracle is as simple as the preparations at the foot of this page, and our new Yardley beauty regime. For these formulae have been perfected to fulfil each office of the complexion . . . cleansing, nourishing, stimulation, with a minimum of time and trouble. And, if you, too, will use snowy English Complexion Cream or Liquefying Cleansing Cream — sparkling Toning Lotion — rich, nourishing Skin Food (basic preparations in our effective, retexturing youth-restoring treatments for dry, aged, normal or oily skins)—we think you will discover the same change to glowing loveliness in your own face this very summer.

Our delightful Yardley preparations are used all over the world, you know, so you'll find them far from costly here in England. Come to our Bond Street Salon for a detailed analysis of your own skin (without charge) and a Yardley skin routine. Or send for our free book, in full colour, "Beauty Secrets from Bond Street," which will tell you just which lovely things to use and the new method of using them. Post us a card today.

FOR SKIN CARE: English Complexion Cream cleanses and nourishes normal skins, 3/6 (triple size 7/6); Liquefying Cleansing Cream cleanses pores, removes make-up, 3/6 (triple size 7/6); Toning Lotion removes cream, stimulates all skins, 2/6 (triple size 5/6); Skin Food nourishes, rejuvenates, 3/6 (triple size 7/6); Skin Lotion, for arms and neck, 2/6 (triple size 5/6); Foundation Cream, 2/6; Trial Beauty Boxes for each type of skin, 5/6. FOR MAKE-UP: Rouge Cream, 2/-; Lipstick, 3/-; Eyeshadow, 2/-; and Nail Enamel, 1/6.

YARDLEY, 33, OLD BOND STREET, LONDON, W.1

In contrast, a 1935 Cutex advertisement ILLUSTRATION 10 shows not only the products, but the glamorous woman applying the lipstick and the four shades available in a frieze above the caption 'Today Your Lipstick Must Match Your Nail Polish'. This slogan was ahead of Revlon's 1940s advertising campaign, carrying the same message. Elizabeth Arden's colour harmony had become Cutex's 'perfect harmony' with no more clashing of nails and lipstick.

Two black and white advertisements for Yardley's products show models in very different settings. In the 1936 advertisement ILLUSTRATION 11 a young woman appears to be in a film set, looking beautiful but turning away from the man. The main caption and to some extent the copy explains the advertisement's meaning, but the underlined line 'There are no more old or ugly women' reinforces the message that women wishing to look young and beautiful should use these products.

ILLUSTRATION 12

Punch, 1938

.... WITH OF COURSE *Yardley Lavender*

When setting out on gay adventures by air sea or land, the lovable fragrance of the Yardley Lavender is indispensable. It adds charm and comfort to the journey and is delightful too for informal evening wear. Yardley Lavender Soap — the luxury soap of the World — is luxuriously scented with the same beautiful fragrance. Its soft mellow lather refines and beautifies the skin and is a beauty treatment in itself.
Lavender from 2/6 to 42/-. Soap in boxes of 3 tablets 2/6. Lavender Face Powder 2/-. Talc 2/6. Bath Salts 2/6.
Yardley, 33 Old Bond Street, London, W.1.

Nowadays this claim would not be allowed. In the 1938 Yardley advertisement ILLUSTRATION 12 the glamorous woman is shown after her sea plane journey, wearing Yardley's lavender soap 'a beauty treatment in itself'. Since air travel in the 1930s was very expensive and the woman is travelling alone, this is a very daring advertisement for its day. Both these advertisements include

the products, though being in black and white, they have less visual impact than the Cutex advertisement.

Another cosmetics company advertising its products to make women look younger was Cyclax, founded in 1897. To celebrate forty years of its existence, the 1937 Cyclax advertisement ILLUSTRATION 13 uses an image of a

Charming women, dangerously attractive, graced the Edwardian courts and . . . went to Frances Hemming of Cyclax for skin care. Because only she could bring flower-like beauty to faces that were innocent of rouge or powder. The young girls who will curtsey to their Majesties this year are going to Lilian Mayle of Cyclax to learn the secret of today's *natural* beauty—the make-up that does not look like make-up. They will learn too, as their mothers learned from Frances Hemming, the simple daily routine that brings clear living beauty into the very tissues of the skin.

TO FILL OUT LINES AND HOLLOWS: CYCLAX SKIN FOOD keeps the skin young . . . definitely eradicates wrinkles. 'Baby' for the very young, 'Thick' for the very lined, Special 'O' for the average skin. Price, 4/-, 7/6

TO CLEAR THE FACE OF SALLOWNESS OR BLEMISHES: CYCLAX SPECIAL LOTION . . . the lotion that is famous for clarifying the skin, drawing out the acid wastes, removing and preventing blemishes. Price, 5/6, 10/6

A POWDER FOUNDATION TO PREVENT DRY SKIN: CYCLAX MILK OF ROSES, a very fine emollient lotion . . . it provides an exquisite powder base for the woman with a dry skin. Price, 4/6, 8/6

TWO POWDER FOUNDATIONS THAT LAST MANY HOURS: CYCLAX DAY LOTION for the dry or normal skin and Cyclax Blended Lotion for the greasy skin, both supplied in matching tones to all shades of powder. Price, 4/6, 8/6

CYCLAX
Famous throughout five reigns

All the best shops throughout the Empire sell Cyclax and will advise on the treatment.
58 SOUTH MOLTON STREET · LONDON · WEST ONE · MAYFAIR 0054
AND 7 EAST 53rd STREET · FIFTH AVENUE · NEW YORK

ILLUSTRATION 13

Harper's Bazaar, 1937

ILLUSTRATION 14

Britannia and Eve, 1939

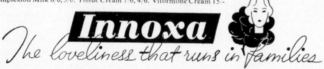

Doctors
recommend
INNOXA POWDER
15 shades 3/6
INNOXA MOUSSE DAY CREAM
3/6, 2/-

HER SKIN WILL BE LOVELY
ALWAYS (LIKE HER MOTHER'S)

But only with Innoxa

She's lovely now and always will be. Innoxa
Rouge and Powder add delicate brilliance to her natural skin tones. Her
powder base . . . Mousse Day Cream . . . is infinitely protective . . . it holds
powder firmly and invisibly . . . and it will cherish her skin for ever. She
has used Complexion Milk since childhood, and Skin Food too. At thirty
she will use Tissue Cream, and at forty, Vitormone . . . as her mother does
today. And that is why her skin will never line or wrinkle.

Complexion Milk 6/6, 3/6. Tissue Cream 7/6, 4/6. Vitormone Cream 15/-

Innoxa
The loveliness that runs in families

FREE. *The truest, most exciting, most romantic, book on beauty ever
written. Send for it to Innoxa Salon, 38 Old Bond Street, W.1*

stylised woman's face – like a mask – highlighting the lipstick, foundation and red nail varnish. It is not clear whose hands they are. Cyclax promoted the idea of young girls' natural beauty make-up that did not look like make-up. (This idea of the natural look reappears in the 1960s). To emphasize how good the products were, it states that they were 'sold in all the best shops throughout the Empire'.

GUERLAIN

LIPSTICK

DARCY

The subject of a mother and daughter, who both use the same cosmetic products, is apparent in a 1939 Innoxa advertisement ILLUSTRATION 14. Dressed up for going out, the mother looks lovingly at her daughter (both look similar in age), who uses the same Innoxa products. This advertisement includes an early mention of a medical reference to the worth of cosmetics, namely 'Doctors recommend'. Later in the century more cosmetics advertisements would include 'scientific evidence' to sell products.

An unusual example of an advertisement targeted at women wanting to 'catch a man' is one for Guerlain lipstick (1937) ILLUSTRATION 15. A simple black and white line drawing of two faces, with the woman wearing bright red lipstick, makes for a very sexy yet artistic advertisement. Another Guerlain advertisement of the same year shows the company selling fantasy, both advertisements having been drawn by Darcy[1] ILLUSTRATION 16.

Mention must be made also of Revlon, founded in 1932 by Charles Revson, which would become a leader in the cosmetics and advertising industries from the 1940s to the present day. This was due mainly to the company spending a larger annual percentage on its advertising budget than any of the other cosmetic companies. For example in 1944 Revlon's advertising budget was $600,000 which had grown to $169 million in 1979.

[1] French illustrator for Guerlain perfumes and cosmetics active from the 1930s to the 1950s.

Reproduced courtesy of Guerlain

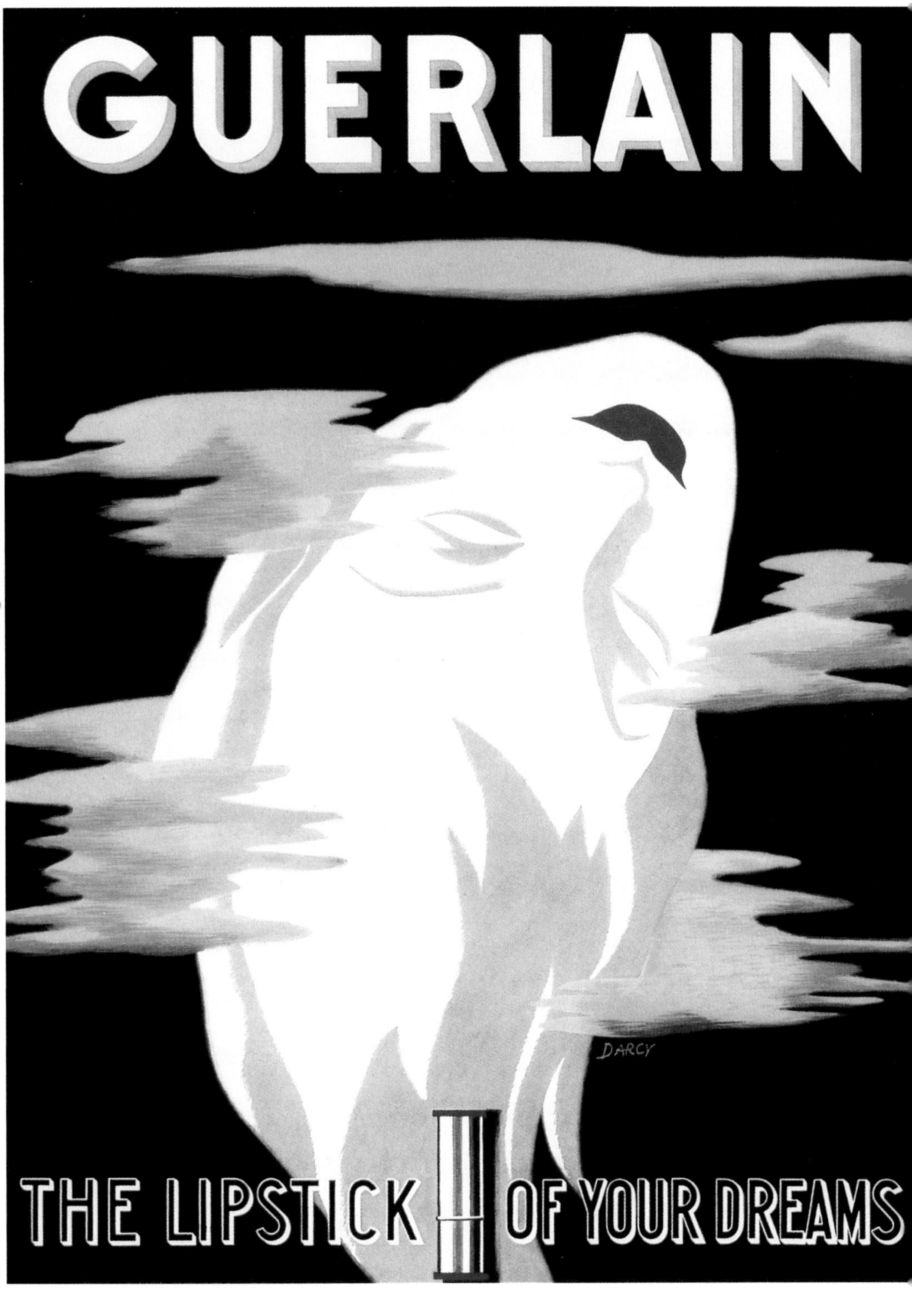

GUERLAIN
DARCY
THE LIPSTICK OF YOUR DREAMS

ILLUSTRATION 16
1937

Chapter 3

1940s

Morale and make-up

During the Second World War in Britain and later in America, the use and advertising of cosmetics was a major method of propaganda and was considered part of the war effort. Women were encouraged to wear cosmetics (mainly lipstick and foundation) to look their best and boost morale at home and abroad for the troops. Whereas cosmetics use and advertisements in America were heavily promoted, in Britain the cosmetics industry was greatly reduced in size for the duration of the war, as industries were given over to munitions and this, combined with a shortage of newsprint, meant that there were few cosmetics advertisements in contemporary magazines.

Two advertisements which illustrate cosmetics being used to boost morale during this period, are Yardley's 'Put your best face forward' ILLUSTRATION 17 and Cutex's 'Woman Power 1943' ILLUSTRATION 18. The first has an image of a woman in the forces, who is positively encouraged to wear make-up, because 'good looks and morale go hand in hand' and by implication would help win the war. In the Cutex advertisement, both the products and the woman's various socio-economic roles are shown – she works in a factory, is also in uniform and yet relaxes in the evening with a man in uniform. The message 'Your war busy hands can be lovely' is clear – even though you are doing your bit for the war effort, you can still be glamorous, if you wear these Cutex products.

Put your best face forward . . .

War jobs leave little time for beauty ritual, but good looks and good
morale go hand in hand. So make up your mind to put your best face
forward every day; to see that your mirror reflects your faith in victory.
Yardley Complexion Powder gives you a natural loveliness
that is completely in the picture nowadays. And its delicate perfume
is perfectly attuned to our new ways of life.

★ *With tax, Yardley Complexion Powder costs 4/-. Look for*
the familiar packing, but remember that though Yardley
beauty-things sometimes wear wartime dress, they still have
all the qualities you know and trust.

Yardley

ILLUSTRATION 17

1943

ILLUSTRATION 18

Chatelaine, 1943

At the end of the war, with rationing still in place in Britain, there was a slow return to cosmetics advertisements in British women's magazines. The advertisements were aimed at putting glamour and normality back into women's lives. A 1945 Cyclax advertisement ILLUSTRATION 19 explains that times of plenty for cosmetics are on their way, by showing a dove of peace and silhouette of a hand representing possibly the evils of war, though the exact meaning of the advertisement is not immediately obvious.

In America, a Revlon advertisement from the same year offers a very different image of a more feminine, glamorous and independent woman wearing Revlon's matching nail varnish and lipstick ILLUSTRATION 20. The woman's head and shoulders are repeated to emphasise the explosive 'Dynamite' colour of the products displayed at the top of the advertisement and the message was – the war is over so let's celebrate.

Max Factor continued to use Hollywood stars, such as Joan Crawford and Judy Garland to endorse his products as can be seen in a 1943 advertisement 'There is only one' – by implication his Pan-Cake Make-Up and Judy Garland ILLUSTRATION 1a (see page 5). This shows an ordinary woman in different vignettes (including in uniform), whilst associating it with the star of the MGM film the 'Harvey Girls', released the same year.

Peace will one day again be a synonym for plenty. Already the most difficult days lie behind us and the time is near when all the Cyclax preparations you desire will be once again in abundance. As their precious ingredients become obtainable and restrictions are eased, so will Cyclax preparations be available to safeguard the birthright of every woman—a lovely complexion.

CYCLAX OF LONDON

58, South Molton Street   Mayfair 0054
New York   Melbourne   Wellington N.Z.   Johannesburg

ILLUSTRATION 19

Vogue, 1945

Smart women knew at once this was the one red they'd
always wanted...sensed that while each of Revlon's
21 color originals in Nail Enamel and Lipstick
had caused a furore...a red like this
was simply *dynamite!*
Sheer Dynamite Face Powder?
Sensational!

Another color triumph by Revlon..."DYNAMITE!"

ILLUSTRATION 20

1945

The theme of the more sophisticated post-war woman
looking for a man (shortages of men after both
wars contributed to the success of such advertising
campaigns) is illustrated in a 1946 Cutex advertisement,
with the copy ' Put it on your long temptress nails...wear
it – then let men beware!' Although woman as the
temptress appears throughout the cosmetics advertising
history, in this advertisement it is tempered by the fact
that she is wearing a ring (not wedding) on her marriage
finger **ILLUSTRATION 21**. Advertising for lipstick became
more sexy and suggestive as can be seen in Elizabeth
Arden's 1948 advertisement for Red Cactus and Desert
Pink (lipsticks were originally red, red or red)
ILLUSTRATION 22.

It's dark...it's exciting...it's the new Cutex color for intrigue. Put it on your long, temptress nails...wear it—then let men beware! • And when in lighter mood try the new Cutex Proud Pink.

ILLUSTRATION 21

1946

ILLUSTRATION 22

1948

Elizabeth Arden

Red Cactus ...

The blue-touched splendour of the flowering cactus caught in radiant colour . . . to enhance the charm of a brunette . . . to be worn with black, white and all shades of blue, wine and grey.

Desert Pink ...

The glory of an Arizona sunset captured in colour . . . to make blonde beauty even lovelier . . . to be worn with black, white, yellow-pink, all shades of green and brown.

RED CACTUS and DESERT PINK Lipsticks, Refills, Matching Cream Rouge.

ILLUSTRATION 23

1947

POWDER SHADES : Cherub ; Lotus ; Nectarine ; Honey ; Rio ; Sarong. Also face creams, make-up foundations and other preparations.

SEE ALL THE GALA LIPSTICK SHADES AT THE GALA SHOP, 48-49 BURLINGTON ARCADE, PICCADILLY, LONDON, W.1

ILLUSTRATION 24

Illustrated, 1948

The Lady Katherine Gurney says: "Pond's Double-Cleansing ritual has made my skin clearer, softer, smoother. I'm thrilled with my new complexion"

Her lovely complexion has the new fragile look of "Dresden China"

Lovely LADY KATHERINE GURNEY has found the way to give her skin that fragile, cared-for look that is in the news these days. She Double-Cleanses it with Pond's Cold Cream.

Here's what she does : regularly, every night, she smooths snowy Pond's Cold Cream over throat and face, swirling it in dozens of tiny circles. She wipes this off. She "rinses" with more Pond's Cold Cream for extra-cleansing, extra-softening. Wipes off again.

Try it yourself! Pond's Double-Cleansing routine leaves your skin wonderfully clean, soft, and glowing. In the morning, smooth in a film of gossamer-light Pond's Vanishing Cream as a powder base and to protect your skin. Your complexion will

the dainty prettiness that makes Lady Katherine Gurney so outstandingly lovely. Pond's Creams are 5/3, 2/7½, 1/2 in jars : in tubes 2/2½ and 1/2, convenient handbag size. Prices include tax.

In complete contrast was an advertisement for Gala lipstick, which simply showed the range of names and colours of its products, for example Heart Red and Cock's Comb, affordable by a female market, with increased spending power ILLUSTRATION 23. Lipsticks and nail varnishes were given weird and wonderful names by all cosmetics companies so that their brand would stand out from their competitors and women would purchase theirs.

After the War, Pond's, Innoxa and Helena Rubinstein continued advertising their expensive, exclusive products to women using traditional advertising images. In the 1948 Pond's advertisement ILLUSTRATION 24 Lady Katherine Gurney[2] endorsed the same Pond's cold cream first advertised in the early part of the century. Helena Rubinstein's 1949 advertisement 'Plan for a lovely skin' still promoted her exclusive products, but this

2 Lady Katherine Paget, daughter of Sir Charles Paget, 6th Marquess of Anglesey and Lady Victoria Manners, married Lt-Col Jocelyn Gurney in April 1941.

ILLUSTRATION 25
1946

the loveliness that lasts a lifetime

she's 17 . . . and thanking Innoxa for *spotless* loveliness.

she's 35 . . . and still very grateful.

at 50 she's proud . . . of herself and Innoxa.

Innoxa
beauty preparations
from Bond Street, London.

advertisement used a painting of a woman holding flowers to sell the product, with instructions on the three steps to beauty: '**Cleanse** your skin with *Pure Washing Cream* to take away every trace of dust and clinging make-up. ..**Nourish** with *Perfection Cream* to feed the **skin…Tone** in the morning with *Skin Toning Lotion*. It closes the pores and leaves a smooth satin-smooth surface for make-up.'

An example of an advertisement showing older women looking younger is the 1946 Innoxa advertisement, 'The loveliness that lasts a lifetime' showing three cameos of women at seventeen, thirty-five and fifty years of age ILLUSTRATION 25. What is worth noting is how old the fifty-year old looks compared with a modern-day woman of the same age.

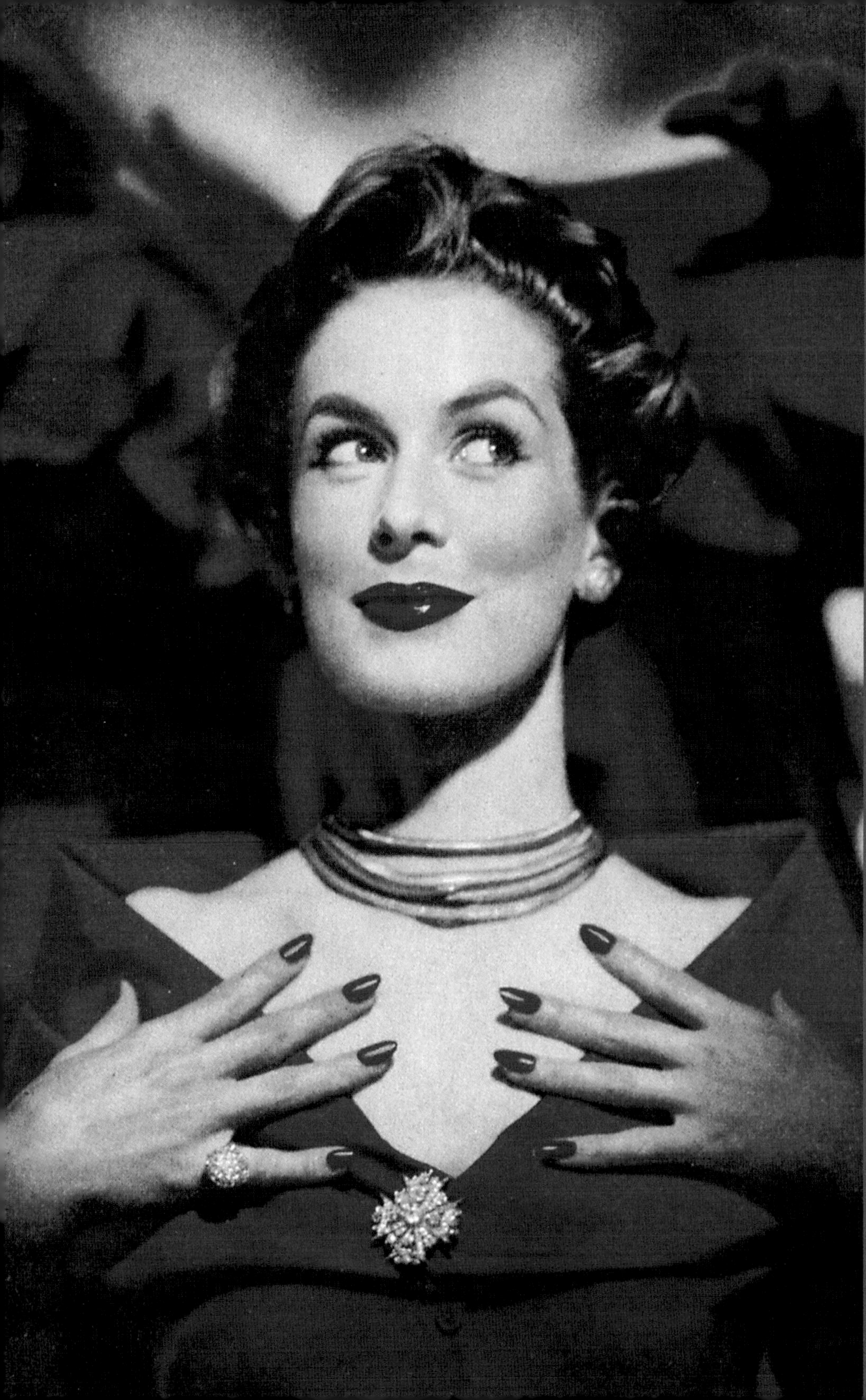

Chapter 4

1950s

Sexual allure

The 1950s in Britain and America was a period of post-war economic recovery and prosperity. The end of rationing in Britain in 1954, including newsprint, led to an exponential rise in the number of women's lifestyle and beauty magazines. During this decade these remained the main avenue for cosmetics advertisements, targeted at single women in the workforce and married or wealthy women with more leisure time and greater spending power. Accompanying these economic and social changes was the increase in the number of mass-produced cosmetic products on the market, leading to fiercely competitive advertising campaigns. There were forty-eight lipstick brands in the mid-1950s and the 'number of cosmetic products from the end of the Second World War to 1980 would fill a book' (Allen, 1981, p.237). Sexual advertising messages became more explicit than in previous decades as it became more socially acceptable to use overt sex to sell products.

Gala, founded in 1938, had retained the same product names in its advertisements but added lip line and nail colour to its range **ILLUSTRATION 26**. To sell the message of the importance of matching lips and nails, the advertisement has a stylised hand wearing red nail varnish and lips of the same colour.

GALA OF LONDON

LIP and NAIL COLOURS

for every fashion shade

LIP LINE
with
interchangeable
refills

NAIL COLOUR
in non-spill
bottle

LIPSTICK
in normal
wind-up case

GALA OF LONDON'S incomparable colours...

each colour identically matched in Lipstick,

Lip Line and Nail Colour...each made specially

to harmonize with the new season's fashion shades.

THE GALA COLOURS ARE:

SEA CORAL	CYCLAMEN
BLAZE	HEAVENLY PINK
CHESTNUT	BALLET PINK
COCK'S COMB	RED BUNTING
LANTERN RED	RED SEQUIN
HEART RED	PRECIOUS RUBY
YOUNG PINK	

GALA OF LONDON

See all the Gala of London Preparations at the Gala Shop, Burlington Arcade, Piccadilly, W.1

ILLUSTRATION 26

1950

ILLUSTRATION 27
1951

Few are born beautiful...
All can achieve beauty
with the Elizabeth Arden Basic Ritual

Keep an inner radiance . . . keep faith with the Elizabeth Arden Basic
Ritual . . . and you will have beauty! Fifteen or fifty — no matter!
Miss Arden's peerless " Essential " preparations will give you swiftly,
surely, the exquisitely cared for look of timeless beauty.

CLEANSE . . . . . *Ardena Cleansing Cream for dry or normal skin, 8/4 to 22/6*
Ardena Fluffy Cleansing Cream for greasy skin, 9/3 to 25/9
TONE . . . . *with Ardena Skin Tonic, 9/3 to 56/9*
NOURISH . . . . *Ardena Velva Cream for young skin, 8/4 to 22/6*
Orange Skin Food for dry skin, 8/4 to 22/6
Ardena Astringent Cream for oily skin, 25/9
Over 30? Ardena Vitamin Cream, 19/3, 30/9

Elizabeth Arden

NEW YORK   25 OLD BOND STREET W.1   PARIS

The two *grandes dames* of the cosmetics industry Elizabeth Arden and Helena Rubinstein continued to promote their luxury products for discerning older women. Elizabeth Arden's 1951 advertisement **ILLUSTRATION 27** states 'Few are born beautiful, all can achieve beauty with the Elizabeth Arden Basic Ritual'. It implies anyone can look this good – 'Fifteen or fifty – no matter!'. The product itself looks old-fashioned as does the stylised, poster-like female figure, reminiscent of those in French nineteenth-century Cheret posters[3]. This is in huge contrast to her Red Riding Hood advertisement of 1948 **ILLUSTRATION 22** (see page 38), which exuded sexiness. The early 1950s saw Elizabeth Arden using exaggerated advertising with her Firmo Lift Treatment Lotion, which claimed it could help you look years younger.

Helena Rubinstein followed suit with her 1950 advertisement 'Word to women who have just passed thirty, the dangerous age for beauty'. According to the advertisement 'sagging contours' can be corrected by using the Contour Lift Film, showing in black and white the head and neck of a woman looking younger. This is an early example of the use of scientific evidence in advertisements promoting cosmetic products.

3 Jules Cheret 1836-1932 French lithographer, poster designer and painter.

ILLUSTRATION 28

1955

YOUNG AS YOU ARE... your skin 'ages' every day

NIVEA puts back
what time takes out

Nivea keeps your skin supple and youthful by replacing the natural oils that time draws from it every day. The secret is that Nivea contains 'Eucerite'—nearest thing in this world to these natural oils. Smooth in Nivea regularly every time you wash your face or hands. Let your mirror be the judge of how much younger, how much lovelier, your skin looks. Whatever your age, Nivea is the one essential cream that your skin needs every day of the year.

SKIN needs NIVEA

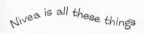

Nivea is all these things

POWDER BASE · NIGHT CREAM
CLEANSING CREAM · HAND CREAM
BABY CREAM · SUN CREAM
SOOTHING CREAM
SPORTS CREAM · MAN'S CREAM

*Nivea Creme in tins 1/4 and 2/3
—or its liquid counterpart
Nivea Skin Oil 2/3 and 4/3*

Nivea also targeted its advertising at these women, as can be seen in the 1955 advertisement of a stereotypical white Anglo Saxon mother and child **ILLUSTRATION 28**. The message is – if you use Nivea daily you too can remain looking young.

At the other end of the 1950s advertising spectrum was Revlon's 1952 'Fire and Ice' campaign **ILLUSTRATION 29** acknowledged by the advertising industry as the most successful campaign in the history of cosmetics advertising. It used for the first time a known fashion model, Dorian Leigh, and changed the accepted American image of a stay-at-home woman into a sexy European temptress, seen first in the 1940s advertisements. It was Charles Revson who was the first to 'realize the marketing benefits that could accrue when the public could identify a range of products with a particular model', rather than just by using Hollywood stars (Allen, 1981, p.254). The illustration is from UK Vogue, March 1953, where the quiz words have been changed for the British market, but the model still exudes femininity and sensuality. As the advertisement states 'Wear it tonight (i.e. the Revlon Fire and Ice lipstick and nail varnish) and it may be the night of a lifetime!'

ILLUSTRATION 29

Vogue, 1953

for you who love to flirt with fire...

who dare to skate on thin ice...

Revlon's 'Fire and Ice'

for lips and matching fingertips. A lush-and-passionate scarlet

like flaming diamonds dancing on the moon!

"Indelible-Creme" Lipstick...Regular Lipstick
and Nail Enamel...
Lastint-ved-Formula Nail Enamel

AVAILABLE BY KIMA
CERT BY ADRIAN MANN

ARE YOU MADE FOR 'FIRE AND ICE'?

Try this quiz and see!

What is the English girl made of? Sugar and spice and everything nice? Not since the days of the Gaiety Girl! There's a *new* English beauty . . . she's tease and temptress, siren and gamin, dynamic and demure. Men find her slightly, delightfully baffling. Sometimes a little maddening. Yet they admit she's *easily* the most exciting woman in all the world! She's the 1953 English beauty, with a foolproof formula for melting a male! She's the "Fire and Ice" girl. (Are *you*?)

Have you ever danced with your shoes off?	*yes* ☐	*no* ☐
Did you ever wish on a new moon?	*yes* ☐	*no* ☐
Do you blush when you find yourself flirting?	*yes* ☐	*no* ☐
When a recipe calls for *one* dash of bitters, do you think it's better with *two?*	*yes* ☐	*no* ☐
Do you secretly hope the next man you meet will be a psychiatrist?	*yes* ☐	*no* ☐
Do you sometimes feel that other women resent you?	*yes* ☐	*no* ☐
Have you ever wanted to wear an ankle bracelet?	*yes* ☐	*no* ☐
Do sables excite you, even on other women?	*yes* ☐	*no* ☐
Do you love to look *up* at a man?	*yes* ☐	*no* ☐
Do you face crowded parties with panic— then wind up having a wonderful time?	*yes* ☐	*no* ☐
Does gypsy music make you sad?	*yes* ☐	*no* ☐
Do you think any man *really* understands you?	*yes* ☐	*no* ☐
Would you streak your hair with platinum without consulting your husband?	*yes* ☐	*no* ☐
If tourist flights were running, would you take a trip to Mars?	*yes* ☐	*no* ☐
Do you close your eyes when you're kissed?	*yes* ☐	*no* ☐

Can you honestly answer "yes" to at least eight of these questions? Then *you're* made of "Fire and Ice"! and Revlon's lush-and-passionate scarlet was made just for you—a daring projection of your *own* hidden personality! Wear it tonight. It may be the night of your lifetime!

ILLUSTRATION 30
1957

Another example of Revlon's blatantly sexy women wearing matching lipstick and nail varnish was a 1957 advertisement for 'Persian Melon' lanolite lipstick **ILLUSTRATION 30**. Compared with the 1952 model, this one is placed in an exotic setting of birds and materials and is giving a very seductive come hither look. Wear this product and you too could 'catch your man'. As a contrast, a Cussons Imperial Leather soap advertisement of 1958 **ILLUSTRATION 31** with two people dancing, full of bright colours and movement, illustrates that the sexy tango can be used to sell something as ordinary as soap.

ILLUSTRATION 31

Vogue, 1958

The Tango 1890

The music of Latin America—evocative of the Spanish gipsy with his guitar and the flamenco singer in her flounced skirt. How stirring, this pulsing rhythm of the Argentine that even today holds a woman close to a man's heart. Her cheek is nearly touching his and he can *see* how soft and sweet it is. Another skin made lovely by the bland, super fatted lather of IMPERIAL LEATHER SOAP.

Cussons
IMPERIAL ⊕ LEATHER

Luxury Soap and Talcum Powder

TOILET SOAP 11ᴰ· · TALCUM POWDER 2/9

"HOW TO BECOME A POPULAR PARTNER" is the title of a fascinating booklet by Alex Moore. If you would like a copy, send your address and 3d in stamps to Cussons Sons & Co. Ltd., 84 Brook St., London W.1.

BATH SOAP 1'9 · BATH CUBES 6ᴰ · AND THE FAMOUS MEN'S TOILET LUXURIES

ILLUSTRATION 32

1956

QUICK! QUICK! QUICK!

Photographed at Los Angeles airport in conjunction with TWA

Creme Puff – that's enough!

No other make-up brings you such complexion loveliness in seconds

In beautiful
Mirror Compact
with
luxury puff

8/3

Refill with
luxury puff

5/6

Fifteen seconds to make-up. Five seconds to touch up. Quickly, quickly, a lasting new loveliness is yours . . . the flawless loveliness that only Creme Puff can bring. Only Creme Puff is beauty-blended . . . a unique combination of powder and lanolin-rich creams, blended to super smoothness. Creme Puff never dries your skin . . . never changes colour . . . always feels fresh and light and always looks so very naturally lovely.

How simple now your beauty routine! Choose today from Max Factor's true-to-complexion shades.

MAX FACTOR

Creme Puff

GUARANTEE. Buy Creme Puff and use according to directions. If you don't agree that you look lovelier than ever before, *the very first time you use it*, simply return the unused portion to Max Factor, Hollywood and London (Sales) Ltd., 16 Old Bond Street, London, W.1, for full refund. * CREME PUFF (trademark) means Max Factor Hollywood creamy powder make-up.

ILLUSTRATION 33
1959

MAX FACTOR
whips up Creme Puff

always ready to flatter your face
with just a breath of color

Only compact make-up with shades so delicately blended they match each individual complexion. Creme Puff never changes on your face. Ends "color-patching" forever!

Just the breath of color you desire ... any time ... any place ... *yours* with Creme Puff by Max Factor. Your choice of nine true-skin tones — blended for each type of complexion as only Max Factor can. And Creme Puff Make-Up never streaks, never changes color — *ends "color-patching" forever!*

IVORY COMPACT ... 1.25*. GOLD-TONE COMPACT ... 2.25*. REFILLS ... 85c*
*PLUS TAX

Max Factor ... *Master of Make-Up Artistry For 50 Years*

Advertisements showing 1950s women at work wearing cosmetics include the 1956 example by Max Factor: 'Quick! Quick! Quick!' **ILLUSTRATION 32**. The message is clear – Max Factor make-up can be applied just before you start work as an air hostess, one of the few 'respectable' careers for women at this time. A 1959 advertisement **ILLUSTRATION 33** shows a woman in her leisure time applying the same Max Factor Creme Puff to go out and socialise (pearls are de rigueur when visiting an art gallery) and to play golf. This is soft and sweet and anything but sexy compared with the previous Revlon advertisements.

ILLUSTRATION 34
1954

It's America's creamiest, longest-lasting lipstick!

Stay Fast stays on hours longer! Stays on after eating,
smoking, even kissing! And thanks to creamy "Moisturizing
Action," Stay Fast keeps lips smoother, softer. Choose from
the prettiest, most kissable colors ever created! For matching
fingertips, try longer-wearing Chip-pruf Cutex! Just 25¢.

Why pay more . . .
when Stay Fast is only
59¢ or **29¢**
Prices plus tax

CUTEX *Stay Fast* **LIPSTICK**

NEVER LEAVES A KISSPRINT

ILLUSTRATION 35
1957

A NEW KISS LIPSTICK

Singing Pink by Goya

A pink to put
a double beat
in his heart

A thrilling pink, an adorable
pink—true not blue, in the
wonderful Kiss texture.
Stays on till you take it
off. Never dries, smears
or changes colour. Glossy,
glamorous lips—*always*.
Enjoy Singing Pink today.

Pink and
gold swirl case **4/6**

Cocktail Case **3/6**

GOYA · LONDON · PARIS · NEW YORK

As competition amongst the cosmetics companies intensified, each continued to develop and advertise the same basic products but increasingly with 'unique selling points' (USP). In 1954 a Cutex advertisement **ILLUSTRATION 34** for its 'creamiest longest-lasting lipstick', shows a glamorous temptress in a red dress, wearing sexy red lipstick and nail varnish, emphasised by the red devil in the background looming over the model. Cutex's Stay Fast lipstick claimed to stay on 'after eating, smoking, even kissing!' Pond's new lipstick used similar copy –

'There's something devilishly delightful about when Pond's Ever So Red is on your lips. No wonder they fight over you!' showing an image of two men fencing over the woman.

Goya claimed also that its 'Singing Pink' lipstick would 'stay on till you take it off' in its 1957 advertisement **ILLUSTRATION 35** showing the traditional image of the head and neck of a glamorous seductive woman, looking like a film star, tempting the man standing behind her.

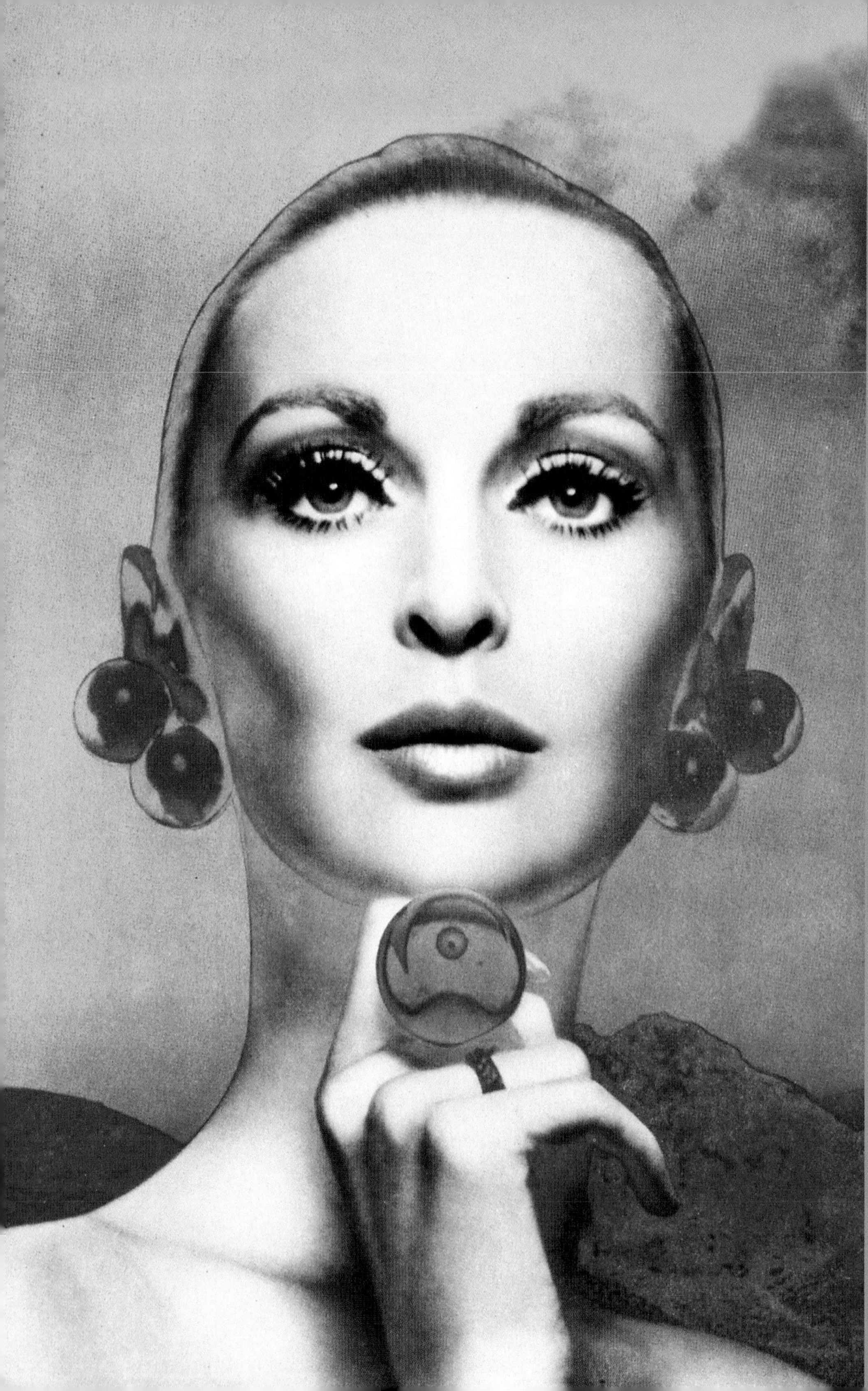

Chapter 5

1960s

Swinging Sixties:
bare essentials

The 1960s was a time of enormous social and cultural changes – in music, in fashion, and to a lesser extent even in the cosmetics industry. It was a time of rebellion and the start of the women's liberation movement. Women were not only living longer but they had become fully independent in the workforce for the first time with the arrival of the contraceptive pill. This produced a more affluent market of consumers with increased spending power and leisure time. Women used cosmetics in this decade more for decoration, especially in the Swinging Sixties referred to in history books as the time of 'sex, drugs and rock n' roll.' There was a proliferation of women's magazines on the market, containing even more cosmetics advertisements, aimed at women wishing to buy into the Sixties culture. All advertisements displayed the same basic products of the previous decades but now with a greater promotion than before of eye shadows.

In the early part of the Sixties, advertisements continued to contain the glamorous and temptress images of the 1950s, aimed at women still trying to get their men. Revlon's 'Touch & Glow' advertisement of 1961 **ILLUSTRATION 36** shows a man and a woman in a very romantic fantasy setting, having a candlelit dinner outside, bearing the caption 'Why tell him it's make-up, he's convinced it's you'. This combination of romantic outdoor setting with female temptress is also illustrated in Cutex's 1965 advertisement **ILLUSTRATION 37** 'Lethal lipstick

WHY TELL HIM
IT'S MAKE-UP...
HE'S CONVINCED
IT'S YOU

And it *is* you...
your complexion
perfected by the
lasting loveliness
of delicate color.
Just choose *your*
shade from thirteen
beautifully blended
'Touch-and-Glow'
skin tones...and
watch the lovely
new glow come over
your complexion.

**Luxurious Liquid Make-Up
Matching Face Powder
Pressed Powder Compact**

'Touch & Glow' by Revlon

Gown by Pierre Balmain for Bergdorf Goodman   Jewels by Van Cleef & Arpels

© Revlon, Inc., 1961

ILLUSTRATION 36

1961

MAN·EATING COLOURS
by CUTEX

ILLUSTRATION 37
1965

Lethal lipstick colours that strike right to his heart

WARNING : Only for girls who like to live dangerously !
New Cutex Lipstick colours that will let you go
Spring Heart-hunting. Wild Temptation to lure,
Torrid Peach to stun, Captivating Coral for the
capture and Pagan Pink for the kill . . . . . .
Cunning colours no man can resist.

**CAPTIVATING CORAL · PAGAN PINK
TORRID PEACH · WILD TEMPTATION
WITH TONING CUTEX NAIL POLISH**

*Unique
easy-slide action
lipstick case*

colours that strike right to his heart'. A model looking like Marilyn Monroe wishes to entice the man away by using Cutex 'cunning colours no man can resist'. The custom of giving cosmetic products ever more nonsensical names can be seen here with 'Torrid Peach' and 'Pagan Pink'.

Another Cutex advertisement of a year earlier ILLUSTRATION 38 suggests that there are two sides of a young woman – introvert and extrovert – using new colours by Cutex. The shy woman on the left contrasts with the extrovert on the right wearing shocking Vixen Red products. The hairstyles and clothes reflect clearly the 1960s fashions.

ILLUSTRATION 38

Vogue, 1964

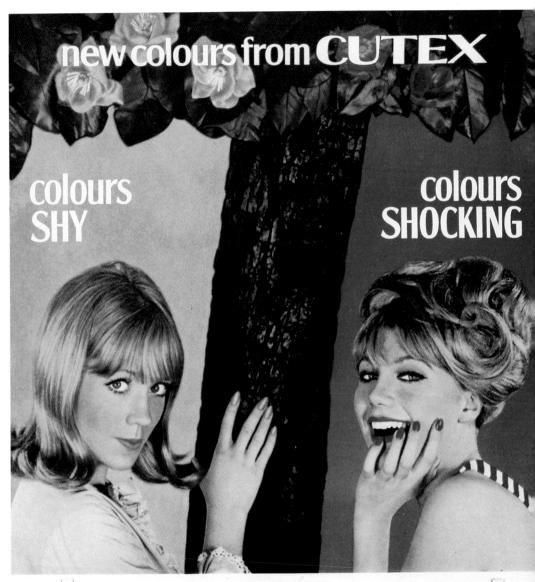

new colours from **CUTEX**

colours
SHY

colours
SHOCKING

Be bashful—be bold—bewitching with the newest **Shy and Shocking Colours by Cutex.** Sheer, clear lights—bold, brilliant brights—to match you mood for mood . . . impulse by impulse—with the Cutex colour collection, so instinctively female you'll want every Shy and Shocking Shade of it. Four natural beauties that flirt as they flatter. Who created this flattery? Why, Cutex, of course! **CUTEX**

SHY:
Nearly Pink, Almost Apricot

SHOCKING:
Red Gone Bright, Vixen Red

KEEP THIS NAME ON YOUR LIPS—

Estée Lauder's

RE-NUTRIV LIPSTICK

CAFÉ

THE RE-NUTRIV COLLECTION: SWISS STRAWBERRY • GRECIAN LILAC • SORRENTO PINK • CAPRI PINK • PORTO FINO ROSE • FRENCH APRICOT • DESERT CORAL
SPANISH MELON • TROPIC TANGERINE • FRENCH PEACH • VALENCIA CORAL • CAFÉ • CASTILIAN • PEPPERMILL • SEVILLA RED • FLORENTINE CHERRY

ILLUSTRATION 39

1964

As in all the previous decades some cosmetics companies opted at times for simpler, understated advertising images, such as Estée Lauder's 'Keep this name on your lips' **ILLUSTRATION 39**. Then there were the advertisements which encapsulated the colourful psychedelic mid to late Sixties of the Beatles Magical Mystery Tour (1967) and the Woodstock Festival (1969). An excellent example of such an advertisement representing this era is Max Factor's 'Bazazz Age Colors' **ILLUSTRATION 40**. The colours, the fashions, the model wearing Bazazzberry Frost lipstick, her hairstyle and earrings of the 1960s all contrast with the conventional packaging of the products on the right.

BAZAZZ! said Max Factor & suddenly Pink went POW! Ginger went SNAP!
Plum came on with a BANG! BAZAZZ! said Max Factor & The Bazazz Age began...

BAZAZZ AGE COLORS!

Kick up your non-heels and come fly with us. You are now entering The Bazazz Age, where the no-mouth is a no-no, and color comes back with a soft, but unmistakable, bang! Four gorgeous color pows: Razabazazz, Bazazzberry, Basic Pinkbazazz, in UltraLucent Creme and Iridescent Lipsticks...and Flash Gorgeous (a Bazazz-y shimmer of pearl that turns pink when it meets your mouth!) At your fingertips, Creme of Bazazz Nail Satin. Four shockingly pale-pretty neutrals that murmur "Bazazz" ever so gently. That's why...Bazazz is. Everything else was.

Bazazzberry Frost on her lips...
Unmatching Creme No. 4
on her fingertips. That's
what Bazazz is all about!

BAZAZZ AGE COLORS by MAX FACTOR

ILLUSTRATION 40

1966

Revlon
invents
the
make-up
that is
and
isn't.

If you can tell you're
wearing make-up, you haven't
got the Look of Today. What's
right now is the 'realskin'
look. Fresh. Natural. (And
soft, soft, soft!)

To give you this 'un-
make-up-y' look, we had to in-
vent our own thing. The first
translucent finish for the
face. A skinny little slip
of colour-in-creme. It even
feels translucent. Slight,
light, layerless. Skin-deep
in moisture. And it looks so
convincing you'd swear it
isn't make-up at all. And it's
not. It's 'Demi Makeup'.

People will think it's
your own fresh, flawless
skin. (Let them.)

Translucent Flowing-Creme. Also:
Pressed Powder/Loose Facepowder/Blush-
ing Powder. In soft, soft demi-shades.

new
'MoonDrops'
Demi
Makeup
invented by Revlon

'MOON DROPS'

REVLON

Also available in the Republic of Ireland

ILLUSTRATION 41

1960s

Charles Revson's constant development and advertising of new Revlon products (usually two new colour ranges each year) resulted in him using contemporary Sixties colours in a two-page advertisement for his new 'Moon Drops Demi Makeup' ILLUSTRATION 41. The colours are very similar to those in the previous illustration but this advertisement shows a more traditional female head shot set against a background of these colours, at the same time highlighting the 'natural' look, which was to be popularised by Mary Quant at the end of the decade.

Eyes can say beautiful things for you!

First . . . Cream Eye Shado, or if you choose to mix and blend shades—Cake or Powder Eyeshado.

Second . . . Eye Liner for contouring Cake or Creamy Liquid, whichever you prefer.

Third . . . Soft Eyeliner Pencil or the Automatic Eye Pencil give eyebrows shape and emphasis.

When you stand back and look at your reflection, your eyes, so sparkling and luminous, will be saying beautiful things for you.

Fourth . . . Eyelash Cosmetique or Mascarette makes beautiful lashes visible.

Fifth . . . Eyelashes, for the fabulous effect you may never have achieved before!

Choose your shades from this palette of colour at your Elizabeth Arden counter.

Elizabeth Arden

NEW YORK · 25 OLD BOND STREET, LONDON W.1. · PARIS.

ILLUSTRATION 42

1966

Even Elizabeth Arden, mainly associated with cosmetics for the top end of the market, used this style in her 1966 advertisement 'Eyes can say beautiful things for you.' ILLUSTRATION 42 to attract younger women to her products. The three faces wearing the eye make-up are set against the same orangey colour, with the products displayed in a practical guide on how to gain beautiful eyes with Elizabeth Arden.

Come on
and make faces—
dozens and
dozens of new
make-up looks
with

NEW FACE KIT

1. **Liplighters.** Pink Plus and Coral Plus
(two vibrant shades) together with Pearl Plus give you
a whole range of lip looks in a 3 in 1 compact palette with
a mirror. **2. Eyelighters.** Eyeliner (for outline)
Brownish Black. Eyelite (for highlight) Pure White.
Eyeshado (for shading and blending) Blue Blue, Turquoise,
Smoky Brown. In a 3 in 1 compact palette with a mirror.
3. Lip and Eye Brush. Double ended. One for eyes,
one for lips. **4. Face Base.** Complete all-in-one make-up.
A subtle cover in real-girl skin tones. Bloom, Beige, Buff.
5. Face Finish Compact. 'No-colour' powder to set your
make-up and give your skin a cool, matt finish.

Face Base

YARDLEY

ILLUSTRATION 43

Vogue, 1967

The change to the method of advertising eye make-up together with lipsticks, can be seen in a 1967 Yardley's advertisement for its New Face Kit ILLUSTRATION 43. The advertisement contains images of lipsticked mouths and multi-coloured eyes, showing a new way of using eye shadow by making eyes more prominent than before.

Christian Dior, better known for its perfumes in the first part of the century, branched out with a full range of cosmetic products, as illustrated in this 1969 advertisement ILLUSTRATION 44. What is new and novel here is the use of the product colours painted over the face to show off the extensive new range of colours.

ILLUSTRATION 44

1969

now
another
New Look
chez
Christian
Dior...

...now a collection of make-up by Dior

colour... more colour... an explosion of colours

ILLUSTRATION 45

Vogue, 1969

Are you going to crack up before you're 45?

However flawless your skin may be now, it can't stay that way for ever without help.

At Guerlain, we don't work miracles overnight.

But we do make a complete course of treatments. And if you use them properly, they'll help keep your face looking young and smooth for years longer than you could normally expect.

The course takes four weeks. And each of the treatments is based on scientific research.

You start with a unique Guerlain product called Hydroserum.

It contains minerals, proteins, lipids and placenta extracts. And they're important to keep your skin vital and alive.

You follow Hydroserum with two special Guerlain creams: Ambrosia Emulsion and Super Nourishing Creme No. 2.

They penetrate deep into your skin, to nourish it and help prevent wrinkles.

When you've finished the course, you should maintain its effect with the Guerlain product most suited to you.

You can buy our treatments in all the finer stores. And you'll find complete instructions inside each pack.

But it's important to first get advice from the store's Guerlain consultant.

If you have any difficulty, call Madame Young at our London salon.

Her number is 01-499 4321.

Guerlain 14 Grafton Street, London, W.1.

Reproduced courtesy of Guerlain

During this period of advertising for the young market, there were still advertisements for the older woman wishing to look younger. For example, the indomitable Helena Rubinstein in her New York home, promoting her 'Beauty Overnight Cream' in a 1960 black and white advertisement. The 'world beauty authority's' claims would probably no longer be permitted under the terms of today's Advertising Standards Authority. One Revlon advertisement read 'Whether you are 25 or 65 (or 75!) your skin can have a youthful beauty never possible before'. Guerlain's advertisement 'Are you going to crack up before you're 45', is another example of the target audience of older women. It contrasted with other advertisements for anti-ageing creams by using scare tactics rather than glamour to get the message across ILLUSTRATION 45.

Possibly influenced by the 1960s Biba[4] fashion look is a 1968 Cyclax advertisement ILLUSTRATION 46 of a stylised sophisticated woman, smoking and wearing the Pearl range of lipsticks and nail varnishes.

4 Biba fashions designed by Barbara Hulanicki, who studied at Brighton Art College and opened her first boutique in Kensington, London in 1964.

ILLUSTRATION 46

1968

GIVE PEARL A WHIRL

Red Pearl   Coral Pearl   Pink Pearl   Orchid Pearl   Coffee Pearl

Shimmer a little this season!

Pick fashion's favourite look for lips
from the Cyclax Pearl range –
five zingy colours with matching nail enamels.

Cyclax
South Molton Street, W.1.

As mentioned earlier, Mary Quant, who revolutionised the packaging and advertising of her cosmetics by appealing to the newly liberated, independent woman, hit the scene at the end of the 1960s. She stressed the 'natural' look (as Revlon had done a few years earlier) as illustrated in the 1968 Mary Quant's Starkers advertisement ILLUSTRATION 47. This advertisement shows a completely naked young woman, her flowing locks covering her nudity with the caption 'To the naked eye it's a naked face… the make-up that looks like it isn't there'. Like the Dior advertisement ILLUSTRATION 44 this was a new and innovative method of advertising cosmetics to the younger market, who could easily identify with this 1960s woman. Mary Quant's products were also very affordable by this younger market.

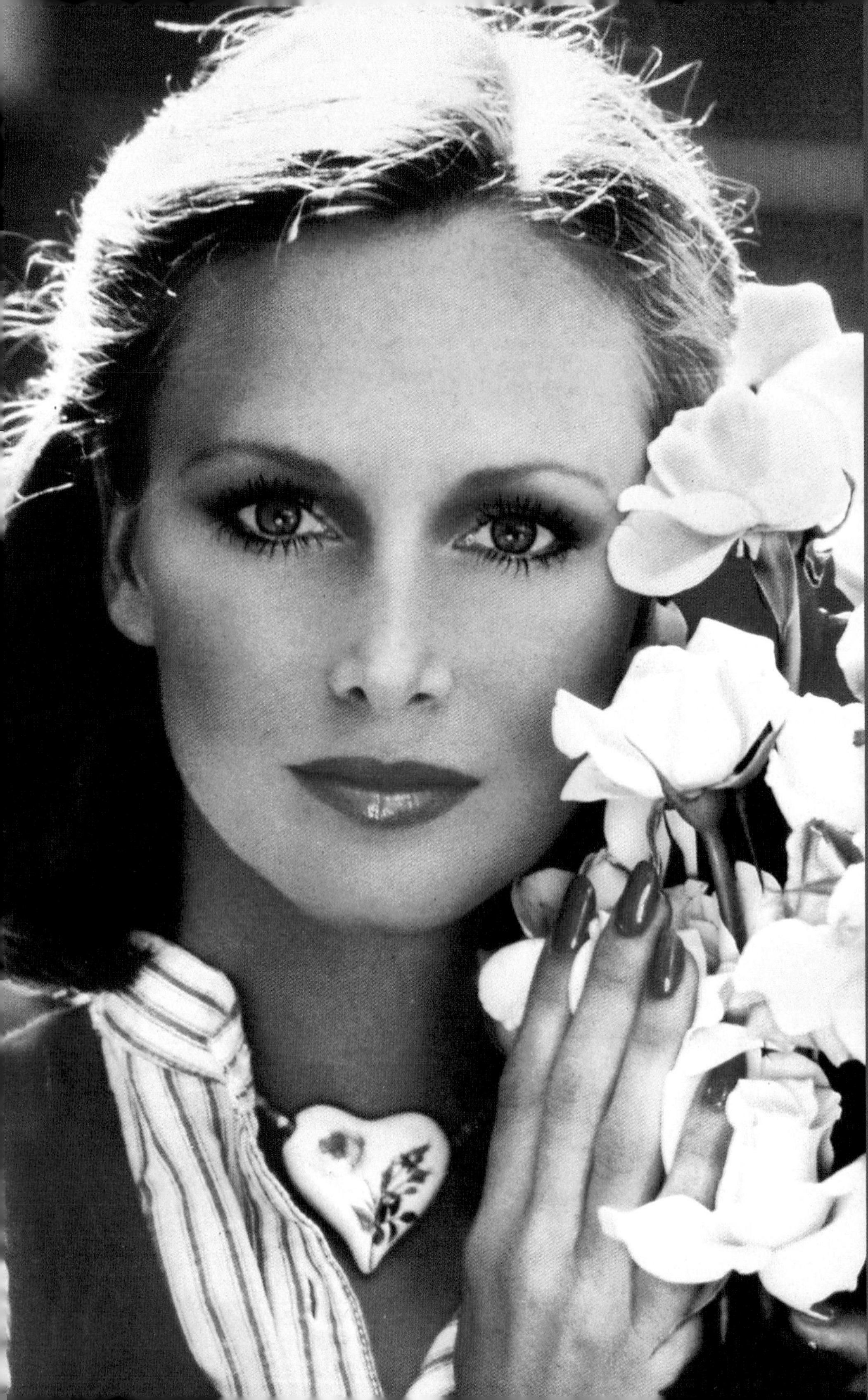

Chapter 6

1970s

Back to nature

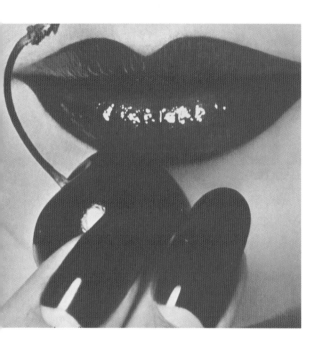

The women's liberation movement, the continued rise in the number of women in the workforce and the growth of feminism with the publication of works like *The Female Eunuch* by Germaine Greer, which challenged the perception of femininity, all made their mark in the 1970s. Initially this caused panic in the cosmetics industry as it did not know whether these 'liberated feminist' women would continue to use cosmetics, because of the old associations of looking beautiful to 'catch a man'. Ardent feminists were anti men and believed that the wearing of cosmetics contributed to the continuing subjugation of woman. Fortunately for both the cosmetics and advertising industries they were in the minority and the majority of 1970s women did still purchase and wear cosmetics as they now wished to express their individuality and look good for themselves. The majority of the 1970s advertisements illustrated here still look very like their predecessors.

Mary Quant's products were very popular as she used old-fashioned natural ingredients and packaged them in new style containers, such as the black and silver Paint Box. In this 1972 advertisement **ILLUSTRATION 48** the natural ingredients of the cosmetics, including honey nuts and beetroot, are juxtaposed with jars of her foundation cream and lipstick. The message is that the products are 'natural' and therefore good for you and will make you look good. Quant also invented new lipsticks and nail varnish colours, which were radically different from any manufactured

"Now you can be a little more natural and a lot more beautiful."

"I've made my new make-up the way it is because everyone should have a chance to buy cosmetics full of natural ingredients."

So says Mary Quant who has packed a pantry-full of nature's ingredients into tubs and bottles to make you more beautiful.

Special Recipe, she's called it. And she's included wheatgerm oil, honey, beeswax, oil of almonds and colours that come from extracts of elderberry, beetroot, carrots and the rich lush greens of leaves and grasses.

The textures are smooth, soft and easy to apply.
The shades are indescribably subtle. They blend wonderfully with your skin.

And sniff the cosmetics. If you're reminded of a spring day and hedgerows, it's no surprise. That's the heady scent of honeysuckle, combined with all the good things Mary insisted on including in her new cosmetics.

Using Special Recipe is like giving your skin a week in the country. Very beneficial.

Which, after all, is the reason why Mary made it.

Mary Quant's Special Recipes.

Only she could have done it.

ILLUSTRATION 48
1972

**"Every girl has a favourite colour.
I have 26," says Mary Quant.**

Quick, think of a colour.
Pale or bright, shiny or muted. Jezebel or Plum Rock,
Ivory or Forever Amber. You name it, Mary has it.
    Not only in her lipsticks, but matching in her nail polishes.
    Whatever the colour is going to be tomorrow, today,
Mary will have it.
    26 in her lipsticks and 26 in her nail polishes. 52 in all.
    How many favourites have you?

Reg'd. Trade Mark. Mary Quant Lip and Nail Colours.
No-one else has them,
because no-one else has Mary.

ILLUSTRATION 49

1970s

Poppy
by
Elizabeth Arden

...sh of red lips against a flawless, translucent skin. Fingertips dipped into a field of wild poppies. A hint
...nflowers in dewy, pearly grass. Your look this spring for cheeks, lips, eyes and nails. By Elizabeth Arden.

...less Finish Cheek Colour · Pearlspun Eyeglaze · Naturally Moist Lipcolour · Salon Formula Nail Lacquer · Conditioning Lash Thickener · Creative Colouring Pencil · Believable Colour.

ILLUSTRATION 50

Vogue, 1977

BEAUTY WISE, VALUE WISE, YOU CAN'T BUY BETTER

ILLUSTRATION 51

Vogue, 1970

before. 'Every girl has a favourite colour. I have 26, says
Mary Quant' **ILLUSTRATION 49**. The brown lips, cherry
and fingernails exude a highly effective sexual message.

The natural look was also promoted by Maybelline,
(target market being the eighteen to thirty-five year olds)
whose eye shadow colours 'borrowed from nature [as]
they don't come any prettier than that'. Daisies, a straw
hat and a blond pretty woman represent how natural
you could look if you used these eye shadows. A different
approach to this natural look can be seen in the 1977

Elizabeth Arden 'Poppy' advertisement **ILLUSTRATION 50**.
'Fingertips dipped in a field of wild poppies' illustrated by
a simple line drawing with make-up areas in colour plus
the product's name 'Poppy'.

Throughout many of the previous decades one
cosmetics company tended to advertise its products very
simply, by showing only the products themselves and
nothing else **ILLUSTRATION 51**. Rimmel's caption 'Beauty
Wise, Value Wise, You Can't Buy Better' had remained the
same, though this was to change in the 1980s.

Nobody minds if your husband looks his age

Men are lucky. They needn't look young to still be attractive. They often get better looking over the years.

Unfortunately, the same can't be said for us women. From the first moment a tiny line appears, we need to take extra care of our skins. With the specialist moisturising treatment, Endocil.

Endocil beauty cream, used every night, will help to nourish and revive your skin.

Light, non-greasy Endocil lotion, used each morning, will protect your skin right through the day.

Together, they'll help you keep its soft, supple beauty years longer. When you don't want everyone to know your age, you'll find your skin can keep a secret. Endocil. All we promise is a lovelier skin.

Photographed at the Albery Theatre, London.

Endocil

ILLUSTRATION 52

1979

Several companies increasingly used scientific evidence and jargon in their advertisements to sell their age-reducing products. Helena Rubinstein's 'The Science of Beauty – smooth away the years with skin life' used GAM 'our exclusive bio-complex', whilst Max Factor had his 'new Swedish Formula Carefree colours to care for your skin'. Endocil implied rather than stated in its advertisements the need for older women to use its products to stop normal signs of ageing as in the 1979 advertisement **ILLUSTRATION 52**. In this scene (in a theatre) the text makes clear the benefits of Endocil cream, but which woman is using it?

Revlon invents
wet lipstick

Here's a beautiful new breed of lipstick. Lush. Liquidy. Mouthwatering. 'Moon Drops' *wet* lipstick makes dry lips a thing of the past. It's literally loaded with lustre, yet the texture is

unbelievably light. *Wet* lipstick almost skims on. (Other lipsticks seem to drag on by comparison.) The feel is fantastic. Like wearing no lipstick at all. And the look is incredible.

'Moon Drops' lipstick

invented by Revlon

ILLUSTRATION 53
1970

Two Revlon advertisements show yet another of Charles Revson's inventions 'Lush. Liquidy... Moon Drops wet lipstick 'ILLUSTRATION 53 worn by a mermaid and the 'Super Rich Mascara with protein', the first mascara, which you could 'bathe in, cry in, sleep in and kiss in!'.

Revlon continued at the same time advertising its more traditional products in a 1973 advertisement **ILLUSTRATION 54** using a head and neck shot showing a confident young liberated woman.

ILLUSTRATION 54

Beauty in Vogue, 1973

Make-up by
REVLON
Left hand page :
Ivory All Weather
Creme Make-up,
Copper All Weather
Creme Blush,
Peacock Blue
& Babie Blue Frost
Super Rich Eye Shadows,
Shy Blue Super Rich Mascara,
Sunfire Flame Lipstick
& Sun Gold Frost Colorshine.
Hair COLORSILK *by Revlon,*
Medium Auburn No. 62

Make-up by
PRINCESS MARCELLA
BORGHESE
This page : Prima Beige I Crema Translucent foundation,
Rosso Cheek Glossa blusher,
Prima Violet & Prima Pearl Crema Shadows,
Smoky Plum Liner Automatico, Notte Mascarola mascara,
Prima Pink II Principessa Lipstick,
Hair COLORSILK *by Revlon, Blue-Black No. 63*

ILLUSTRATION 55

1971

she has that Dior Look...

33 Dior fashion shades
for eye-make-up

Dior eye shadows :
sticks, compacts,
glitter powders

"Long, tapering, scarlet-tipped.
Pure invitation. And red for danger."

Hands. Seen almost as soon as your face.
On show. Touching. Holding. Loving.
Nail polish is as important as make-up.
That's why we call Cutex the make-up for nails.
Thirty different colours. Some dramatic.
Some soft. Some vivid. Some gentle.
More than nail polish. It's make-up for nails.

Cutex

Thirty colours. Some so spectacular they send messages.

ILLUSTRATION 56

Cosmopolitan, 1978

Mystery and danger were themes still used to advertise products as in the 1971 Christian Dior advertisement 'she has that Dior Look', where your attention is drawn to her painted eyes **ILLUSTRATION 55** and Cutex's 1978 'dangerous red nails' **ILLUSTRATION 56**. The image of three fingers with red nails does convey danger, when you interpret them as talons.

Images of financially independent career women began to appear more frequently in 1970s advertisements to represent their presence in the workforce. In the 1976 Estée Lauder advertisement **ILLUSTRATION 57** a woman wearing fashionable clothes is opening the door of her sports car whilst still retaining her femininity as shown in the main part of the two-page spread. Power-dressed women getting to the top of their careers is illustrated in Max Factor's Colorfast New Renaissance advertisement **ILLUSTRATION 58**. The actress Fiona Fullerton demonstrates that if you wear Max Factor's cosmetics you too can be the boss and not just the secretary.

Earth roses. Amethyst roses. Rose roses. Unheard of roses.

Whatever you're wearing this Spring,
wear it with roses. Estée Lauder's new

Runaway Roses.

Fifteen new and different roses for eyes, cheeks, lips, fingertips.
There are rare brown roses. Unexpected garnet roses. Refreshing
rose roses. They're just what Spring's whites, brights and paled
down neutrals need to look new and fresh.
So come, catch the whole bouquet.

Eyes: Pressed Eyelid Shadow in Rose Lilac/Rosy Amethyst,
Rose Star/Garnet Rose.
Lips: RE-NUTRIV Rich Rich Lipstick in Rose Peony,
Rose Carnation, Tawny Rose.
Tender Lip Tint in Strawberry Rose, Romany Rose.
Cheeks: Soft Film Compact Rouge in Rosy Morning, Brandied Rose.
Tender Blusher in Freshwater Rose, Really Rosy.
Fingertips: Lustrous Nail Lacquer in Rose Heather, Café Rose.

Estée Lauder

ILLUSTRATION 57

Vogue, 1976

New Renaissance

GLOWING COLOURS...TO STAY AS BEAUTIFUL AS THE DAY IS LONG.

COLORFAST
LONG LASTING COSMETICS.
BY MAX FACTOR

ILLUSTRATION 58

1970s

It's the latest thing to be seen in.

The latest fashion starts with California.
The brightest, boldest, most compelling make up is here.
Make big flirty eyes with new California Tri-colours.
Three dreamy creamy eye shadows in one neat compact.
Turn on to the amazing new autumn shades for lips
and nails. Bright light colours like Viva Chili for lips or
Silver Glitter for nails.
Everything happens first in California.

ILLUSTRATION 59
1974

California, Another beautiful idea from MAX FACTOR

The use of women of colour to advertise mainstream cosmetic products was not fully developed until the 1990s. The LHA collection does however contain a 1974 advertisement for Max Factor's California range **ILLUSTRATION 59** 'it's the latest thing to be seen in' showing a successful black woman shopping with friends. Nowadays this may seem normal but more than thirty years ago it was very exceptional. It is interesting to note that although the advertisement is set in California, it appeared in a British magazine.

Chapter 7

Having it all

1980s

ritain in the 1980s was dominated politically and socially by the Thatcher era and the 'me' philosophy, which had an influence on the cosmetics and advertising industries. As in the 1970s, women now wore make-up for themselves and not just 'to catch a man'. The majority of the 1980s advertisements reinforced this message of women looking good for their own sakes, especially those in the workforce, having to balance work and family life. Not only was there an even greater variety of cosmetic products on the market, but they were now affordable by all social classes, including the blossoming teenage market. However, advertisements in magazines increasingly had to compete with advertisements on television and in the cinema.

Max Factor's 1982 advertisement 'Don't you love being a woman?' **ILLUSTRATION 60** embodies this message of women decorating their face and hands to look good for themselves. So too does Endocil's 1985 advertisement 'A beautiful face starts with beautiful skin' **ILLUSTRATION 61** which uses images of a woman's eyes, nostrils and nails and not her skin. A more colourful image of a sophisticated working woman is Revlon's 'Rosa di Roma' 1982 advertisement **ILLUSTRATION 62** featuring the Italian actress Isabella Rossellini.

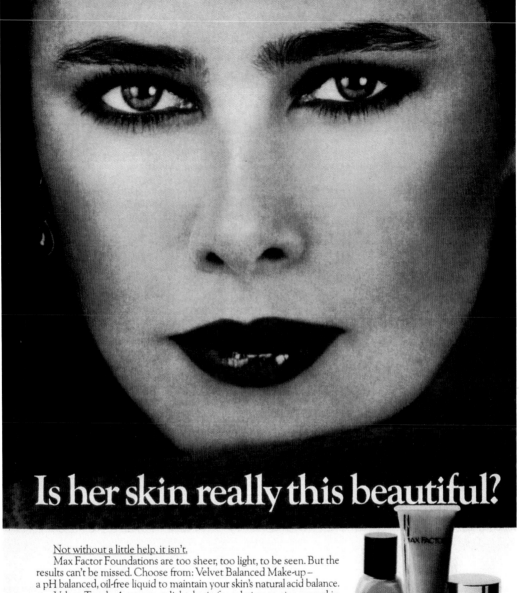

Is her skin really this beautiful?

<u>Not without a little help, it isn't.</u>
Max Factor Foundations are too sheer, too light, to be seen. But the results can't be missed. Choose from: Velvet Balanced Make-up – a pH balanced, oil-free liquid to maintain your skin's natural acid balance.

Velvet Touch. A gossamer light, basic foundation to give your skin a fresh radiant look.

Ultra Moist. A creamy, richly moisturised foundation that's especially kind to drier skins.

Use one of these foundations from Max Factor and they could be asking it of you. Is her skin really that beautiful?

Foundations from

DON'T YOU LOVE BEING A WOMAN?   MAX FACTOR.

ILLUSTRATION 60

Cosmopolitan, 1982

A BEAUTIFUL FACE STARTS WITH BEAUTIFUL SKIN

Endocil moisturising beauty cream provides deep-softening day and night protection for your skin.
One of a range of skin care products to keep you looking beautiful.

ILLUSTRATION 61

Good Housekeeping, 1985

ROSA di ROMA

Colours that Italy knows best how to dress in, live in, and love in.

Tonight...greet the dawn with the silent beauty of exquisite colour. Naturally, they're called Roman Wine, Rosa Romana and Cappuccino ...To love your lips, eyes and nails.

REVLON

ILLUSTRATION 62

1982

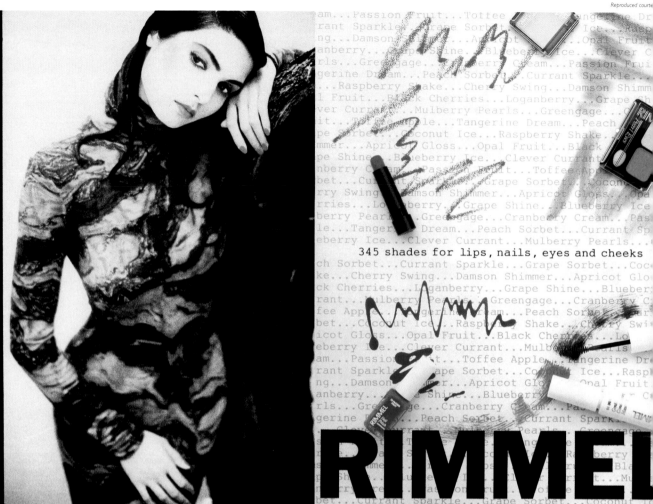

345 shades for lips, nails, eyes and cheeks

RIMMEL

FORBIDDEN FRUITS

ILLUSTRATION 63

Cosmopolitan, 1987

In order to compete more effectively with advertisements in other types of media, some companies employed even more daring and original advertising images. One of the best examples is Rimmel's 'Forbidden Fruits' advertisement of 1987 **ILLUSTRATION 63** which is as different from its 1970 advertisement **ILLUSTRATION 51** as it could be. Rimmel changed hands several times during the 70s and 80s and this may explain the contrast in campaigns. Christian Dior's advertisement of 1985 repeats its

mysterious and glamorous eyes of fourteen years before but adds to the mystery and glamour with its use of the term maquillage (French for make-up) for its autumn colours **ILLUSTRATION 64**. Helena Rubinstein also used the word in a 1982 advertisement labelling her very red lipstick and nail varnish 'le nouveau maquillage'. That image not only had the 'wow' factor, with its bright red background, but contrasted with her earlier advertisements by focusing on visual impact rather than information.

Christian Dior

MAQUILLAGE

LES EXCENTRIQUES

Dark is the night, velvet-dark...A deep and sumptuous back-drop to a little sublime madness – Dior's autumn colours. Dark shadows and troubled mysterious glances, strangely luminescent eyeliner pencils, glittering mascara, unashamed lip and nail colours, and subtle alchemy of the new Blush-Nuances – double play of bright shades softened by a mist of pale powder.

93

ILLUSTRATION 64

Vogue, 1985

THIS SEASON'S
PSYCHEDELIC
SHADES FROM
PERFECT COLOUR.

**A SHOCK OF PINK, A FLASH OF ORANGE, IT'S BEGINNING
TO LOOK A LOT LIKE LUCY IN THE SKY.**

MOD PINK.

TANGERINE DREAM.

MY GENERATION.

HITCHIKER BLUES.

CRAZY CERISE.

FAR OUT.

STOP ON SIGHT.

PINK PERIL.

MINI SKIRT.

OP ART.

PERFECT COLOUR
by CUTEX

AVAILABLE AT BOOTS, LARGE CHEMISTS AND MOST LEADING DEPARTMENT STORES.

ILLUSTRATION 65
1986

Cutex made reference back to the 1960s in its 1986 'Perfect Color' advertisement **ILLUSTRATION 65** for the season's psychedelic shades, which were 'beginning to look a lot like Lucy in the Sky'.[5] By its use of a very young model, this advertisement would have appealed to both teenagers and older women (possibly their mothers) remembering their own youth.

Following on from its successful sales of Charlie perfume in the 1970s, Charles Revson brought out a complete Charlie range of cosmetics in the 1980s aimed specifically at young independent women in the workforce. 'Have you seen Charlie's eyes' is such an advertisement from this period **ILLUSTRATION 66**.

Breaking down barriers for women wishing to work in traditionally male dominated jobs is wittily portrayed in a 1981 Maybelline advertisement. The model is shown holding a pneumatic drill showing off her nail-varnished hands, the implication being that she could drill the road if she wanted to and her Maybelline nail varnish would not get easily chipped.

5 Lucy in the Sky with Diamonds is a track from the Beatles'
Sgt Pepper's Lonely Hearts Club Band album, June 1967

Have you seen
Charlie's eyes?

Charlie

A collection of the most original eye make-ups you ever laid eyes on. Beautifully priced.

ILLUSTRATION 66
1985

DOES YOUNG-LOOKING SKIN SEEM ONLY A DREAM?
Nothing can be so lovely as the delicate blush of perfect, soft skin. Yet sometimes, at the end of the day, that natural freshness may seem just a shade less radiant. It is then that your skin needs the extra nourishment which is to be found in Night of Ulay Enriched Beauty Cream. Before you sleep, you will feel how readily your skin accepts this finely balanced blend of oils and emollients. Rich enough to nourish your skin the night through yet deceptively light and non-greasy. Allowing your skin to breathe even as you sleep.
And at the first touch of morning you will start to feel how Night of Ulay can help you stay young-looking too.

ILLUSTRATION 67
1986

Oil of Ulay, which by the mid-1980s had become the leading supplier of facial moisturiser, took on Elizabeth Arden and Helena Rubinstein's mantle of advertising creams to women wishing to look younger, 'Does young looking skin seem only a dream?' in this 1986 advertisement **ILLUSTRATION 67**. At the same time Helena Rubinstein had her Performance H_2O hydration products and Innoxa its Science and Nature product range, both examples of the continuing use of 'scientific evidence' to sell their products.

Liza Minnelli
Los Angeles, California

The most unforgettable women in the world w

ok.
ustrous eyeshadows with
ew Silkglide Formula.*

ok again.
olors that last so long.
lend so smooth. Stay
• true. (That's no lie!)

ok again. 35 jewel-like
nes to try.
75 combinations for
st 2 eyes.

ok again. A lifetime
f perfect coordination.

USTOM EYES*
om Revlon.

ook again.
nd you'll never look back.

REVLON

ILLUSTRATION 68
1987

Forty years after Max Factor used Hollywood star Judy Garland to endorse his cosmetics, Revlon used her daughter Liza Minnelli in the same way in the 1987 advertisement 'The most unforgettable women in the world wear Revlon' **ILLUSTRATION 68** to advertise its Custom Eyes range of products, which gave women '7175 combinations for just 2 eyes'.

Chapter 8

1990s

Changing faces

The last decades of the twentieth century saw a continuation and further development of cosmetics advertising targeted at the baby boomers born in the 1940s and 1950s, who now formed an increasingly large and lucrative market. Oil of Ulay had its daily renewal cream (the UK's number one anti-ageing cream) and its Pro-Vitalyte cream, the latter endorsed by Diana Moran, 57 (the Green Goddess)[6] as illustrated in an advertisement captioned 'At last a moisturizer designed to help me LOOK how I feel'. Avon's Age Block Daytime Defence Cream uses an image of a woman of colour to advertise its product **ILLUSTRATION 69**. This was a very original idea as many people associated Avon with cosmetics for white people only, though in fact it had started in the 1950s selling to black people in America.

6 British model who wore a bright green leotard to promote health and fitness in the 1980s on BBC TV's Breakfast Time programme.

Dare to
change
your mind about A V O N

AVON
Age Block
Daytime Defence Cream
with UVA/UVB Protection

Time won't tell

So you've got great skin already?
Let's keep it that way. The effects of the environment,
including ordinary daylight, are ageing your skin every
single day - causing around 80% of the visible signs of
premature ageing. **Avon Age Block Daytime Defence
Cream** contains PARSOL® 1789, an advanced UVA
absorbent which helps protect against photoageing.
Take action now and look forward to beautiful skin for
years to come.

As time goes by,
you'll be glad you did.

Leading edge technology from the global
Avon Skin Care Research Centre.

AVON
SKIN CARE
RESEARCH CENTRE

for more information call us on our local rate number.

0 8 4 5   6 0 5 0 4 0 0

http://www.uk.avon.com

For more information and the current Avon Brochure, simply print your details below, send off the freepost coupon, and we'll be in touch.

Name _____ Address _____

Postcode _____ Tel _____

☐ I would like to order direct by phone ☐ I would like to order through an Avon Representative ☐ I would like to know more about becoming an Avon Representative

SEND TO: **FREEPOST**, AVON COSMETICS, NORTHANTS. NN17 4AZ
Residents of Republic of Ireland call 0502 42530

20260   ☐ Please tick this box if you do not wish to receive mailings of offers or services from other carefully selected companies

A V O N

ILLUSTRATION 69

SHE, 1997

ILLUSTRATION 70
Red, 2001

Clarins creates
LE ROUGE.
Boys, are you
ready for this?

NEW. A celebration of life. A celebration
of women. Clarins reinvents lipstick.
Hydration. Protection. Seduction. In 36 shades.

CLARINS
— PARIS —

www.clarins.com

It's a fact. With Clarins, life's more beautiful.

From the beginning of the 1990s and into the twenty-first century, there was an increase in the number of advertisements featuring women of colour, which reflected the increasing racial diversity of British society. Rimmel used the head and neck of a black woman, with one eye closed in its Power Lash advertisement and Clarins used another black woman for its seductive red lipstick **ILLUSTRATION 70**. Hollywood stars, both black and white, appeared in advertisements – Halle Berry endorsing Revlon's Super Lustrous lipstick and Helena Bonham Carter as the face of Yardley **ILLUSTRATION 1b** (see page 6). Cosmetics specifically for women of colour were further developed during this decade, for example Iman's and Maybelline's 'Shades of You' ranges, and with them came the advertising of these new products to a niche market. The real growth of this market has, however, taken place in the twenty-first century.

ILLUSTRATION 71

1997

What kind of Oil of Ulay keeps
your lips looking great for hours
THIS ON

For the past few years we have been proving that our creams
keep your skin looking younger. Now we can prove our lipstick
keeps your lips feeling softer. Introducing new Colourmoist
Lipsticks, the first from Oil of Ulay. And thanks to our colour
enhancers, we can also prove that our lipsticks last. On your
lips. Hour, after hour, after hour. And the name? Colourmoist
Lipsticks, part of our new Colour Collection.

LONG LASTING LIPSTICKS

OIL *of* ULAY

WE CAN PROVE LONG LASTING COLOUR CAN CARE

ILLUSTRATION 72
1998

Advertisements targeted at the teenage market continued to appear in the mass circulation teen magazines such as *Seventeen*, as teenagers had greater spending power. Cosmetics companies wanted to catch them young and keep them brand loyal thus guaranteeing a market for their products for decades. Nivea was no exception with its 1997 advertisement

'Sensational…a new softness for my skin instantly' **ILLUSTRATION 71**. Even Oil of Ulay, famous for its anti-ageing creams, launched its first lipstick 'What kind of Oil of Ulay keeps your lips looking great for hours? THIS ONE', aimed at the younger end of the market **ILLUSTRATION 72**.

Elizabeth Arden

ILLUSTRATION 73

SHE, 1997

At last...
Exceptionally moist.
Exceptionally lasting.

Introducing
Exceptional Lipstick

From the moment it touches
your lips, you know it is
exceptional in every way.

Dior

EXPRESSIONS DE ROUGE

ILLUSTRATION 74

Harpers and Queen, 1997

" Touchproof. It means you can actually forget you're wearing mascara. "

Tim Earnshaw Make-Up Artist 'Titanic'.

MAXFACTOR
The make-up of make-up artists

No. 1 Lash Enhancer.
Natural look.

No. 2. Stretch.
Classic look.

No. 3. 2000 Calorie.
Dramatic look.

Introducing Max Factor's new range of mascaras.
No more smudges. No more panda eyes.

ILLUSTRATION 75
1998

Some things stayed the same in cosmetics advertising during this decade such as the use of beautiful white women to advertise the products. Three examples of this are Elizabeth Arden's 'Exceptional Lipstick' advertisement of 1997 **ILLUSTRATION 73** Christian Dior's of the same year 'Expressions de Rouge' **ILLUSTRATION 74** and Max Factor's new mascara range endorsed by a make-up artist on the Hollywood film Titanic **ILLUSTRATION 75**. Max Factor's Film Noir cosmetics collection is an example of the continued influence of cinema in cosmetics advertising.

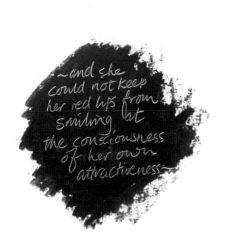

~and she
could not keep
her red lips from
smiling at
the consciousness
of her own
attractiveness~

MADE UP BY LEO TOLSTOY.

ILLUSTRATION 76

1990

MADE UP BY RIMMEL.

Rimmel's 1990 advertisement **ILLUSTRATION 76** included a quote from Leo Tolstoy[7], representing classy nostalgia, placed opposite a stylised mouth and hand being drawn by a red lip liner, with the words 'Not tested on animals' underneath. This was in order to make it clear to animal rights activists, who campaigned relentlessly against the use of animals in testing cosmetics, that Rimmel was a socially aware company.

7 Russian author 1828–1910.

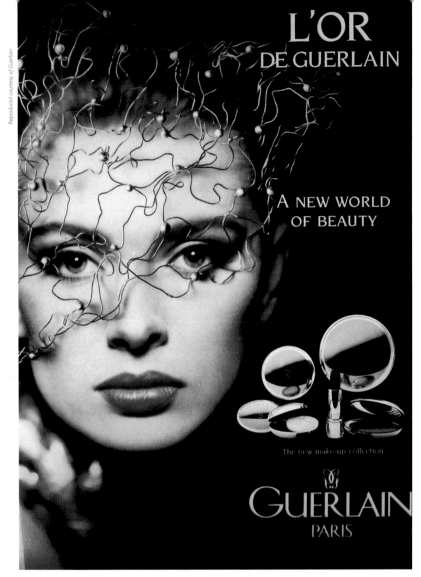

ILLUSTRATION 77

Vogue, 1991

The 1991 'L'Or de Guerlain – a new world of beauty' advertisement **ILLUSTRATION 77** showed a world of luxury and the ultimate in ideal beauty, using the symbolism of gold as the most valuable commodity. The woman's golden complexion comes from the make-up in the gold make-up cases and she is also wearing an expensive, exquisite gold headdress.

This advertisement encapsulates the main purpose of the cosmetics industry throughout the century: to sell beauty and dreams to a market comprising women of all ages and types. Despite the exponential rise and influence of the World Wide Web from the mid-1990s, the cosmetics advertising industry continued to promote its products in women's lifestyle magazines as well as in the other media of television and cinema. As long as women want to look and feel good by using cosmetics, as Rustenholz (2003, p.30) puts it, the advertising industry will continue to promote 'make-up as a means of transforming age and even ugliness into youth and beauty.'

GLOSSARY OF COSMETIC BRANDS

AVON – founded in 1886 by door-to-door salesman, David H McConnell, the original name was California Perfume Company. The name was changed to Avon in 1939 and arrived in Britain in 1959.

CHRISTIAN DIOR – cosmetics division was founded in 1947.

CLARINS – a French family-run business founded by Jacques Courtin-Clarins in 1954 and now sold internationally.

CUSSONS – began as Cussons & Sons in the early 1900s and acquired by Paterson Zochonis (PZ) in 1975. The name was changed to PZ Cussons.

CUTEX – founded in the 1920s and now owned by Coty Inc.

CYCLAX – founded in 1897and acquired by Yardley in 1972. The brand is now owned by Richards and Appleby.

ELIZABETH ARDEN – founded in 1910 in New York and main rival of Helena Rubinstein; still a leader in the beauty and cosmetics industry.

ENDOCIL – originally manufactured by Organon Laboratories, now owned by Keyline Brands, part of the Godrej Group of Mumbai.

ESTÉE LAUDER – founded in 1946 in New York by Josephine Esther Mentzer and her husband Joseph Lauter.

GALA – founded by Stanley Picker in 1938 but now a dormant brand owned by Procter & Gamble.

GOYA – formed in the 1930s and now a dormant brand owned by Coty Inc.

GUERLAIN – founded as a perfume company in 1828 and opened its first beauty salon in Paris in 1938. The company was acquired by LVMH (Moët Hennessy Louis Vuitton) in 1994.

HELENA RUBINSTEIN – opened her first salon in Melbourne in 1903 and went on to open salons in London, Paris and New York. She was famously a rival of Elizabeth Arden. The brand is now owned by L'Oreal.

INNOXA – founded in France in 1920, dissolved as a UK company and products now only available in Australia, New Zealand and South Africa.

MARY QUANT – founded by her in 1966 (with money from Gala cosmetics), she resigned as Director in 2000 after a Japanese buyout; now trading as Mary Quant Cosmetics Japan Ltd.

MAX FACTOR – a family-owned company founded in Los Angeles in 1909; now owned by Procter & Gamble.

MAYBELLINE – founded in 1915 by TL Williams and named after his sister, Mabel and Vaseline, the key ingredient to Maybelline mascara; now owned by L'Oreal.

NIVEA – founded in Germany in 1911 by CP Beiersdorf, which still owns the brand today.

OIL OF ULAY – founded in 1949 in South Africa as Oil of Olay, now owned by Procter and Gamble and known in most countries simply as Olay.

POND'S – originated in 1846 and became an established cosmetics brand in the early 20th century. The brand has been owned by Unilever since 1987.

REVLON – founded in 1932 by Charles Revson, his brother Joseph and Charles Lachman; sold to a subsidiary of MacAndrews & Forbes Holdings in 1985.

RIMMEL – founded in 1834, now owned by Coty Inc.

YARDLEY – dates back to 1620 (soap concession from Charles I) and was, by the 1930s, Britain's leading cosmetics business; now owned by The Lornamead Group

BIBLIOGRAPHY

ALLEN, Margaret (1981) *Selling dreams: inside the beauty business*, J M Dent

BANYARD, Pip (2002) *Because you're worth it: 100 years of make-up*, 2 Videos, 13 and 20 February 2004, Channel 4

COHEN RAGAS, Meg and Karen KOZLOWSKI (1998) *Read my lips: a cultural history of lipstick*, Chronicle Books

DE GRAZIA, Victoria (ed) (1996) *The sex of things: gender and consumption in historical perspective*, University of California Press

DYER, Gillian (1982) *Advertising as communication*, Methuen

ENCYCLOPEDIA (1994) *Encyclopedia of consumer brands, Vol.2 Personal products*, St James Press

GUNN, Fenja (1973) *The artificial face: a history of cosmetics*, David & Charles

KOSMETIK/COSMETICS *Novum Plus*, 2002 January pp.35–49

LURY, Giles (2001) *Brandwatching: lifting the lid on branding*, 2nd ed. revised & enlarged, Blackhall Publishing

MCLUHAN, Marshall (1964) *Understanding media*, Routledge & Kegan Paul

MILLUM, Trevor (1975) *Images of women: advertising in women's magazines*, Chatto & Windus

NEVETT, T R (1982) *Advertising in Britain*, Heinemann

RUSTENHOLZ, Alain (2003) *Make up*, Hachette

SAUNDERS, Dave (1999) *Twentieth century advertising*, Carlton

TELFORD, Anne 'Sex in advertising', *Communication Arts Magazine*, 1997, Vol.39 pt Sep/Oct pp.84–91

TOBIAS, Andrew (1976) *Fire and Ice: the story of Charles Revson, the man who built the Revlon empire*, Morrow

WILLIAMSON, Judith (1981) *Decoding advertisements: ideology, meaning in advertising*, Marion Boyars

WYATT, Tom (1995) 'Making faces'. *Creative Review*, April 1995 pp.30–31